Contents

Bukowski Journal Vol: #1

Editorial 4
Love for $17.50 ~ Luc G. Nicknair 5
A Drunken Sage? ~ A. Monk 11
Steal This book Now! ~ Alexander Goins 14
"I Told You So" ~ Martin Eden 19
Love is a Dog From Hell ~ Michael d. Meloan 23
Introduction to Essay ~ Neil Schiller 27
Social Mechanics & American Morality ~ Neil Schiller ....
Round Peg in a Square Hole ~ Simon Mackie ....
Bukowski on Film ~ Steve Baker ....
Henry Charles Bukowski ~ Michael d. Meloan 1
Terror Street Tapes ~ Miles ....
Drinking The Buk ~ John J Martinez ....
Bukowski & Censorship ~ Wilfred D. Day 110
Books of a Dirty Old Man Part 2 ~ Rikki Hollywood 118
Reviews 133
Cool Contacts! 157

Views expressed in this publication are not necessarily those of the editor, and are for informational purposes only. All illustrations are c owners. Other contents c Bukowski Journal and individual contributors.
We always welcome Bukowski related idea's, suggestions, reviews, artwork but cannot be held responsible for unsolicited items going astray. If it's valuable, send it registered.

Credits

Editor: Rikki Hollywood

Front Cover: Colin Cross & Rikki Hollywood
Back Cover: Colin Cross & Rikki Hollywood

Thanks to our Contributors!
Steve Baker   Simon Mackie
Colin Cross   Michael d. Meloan
Wilfred D. Day   A. Monk,   Miles
Martin Eden   John J. Martinez
Alexander Goins   Luc G. Nicknair
(Big Thanks) **Neil Schiller**

Bukowski Unleashed! "Essays on a Dirty Old man"
Bukowski Journal Vol: #1
ISBN: 0-9535231-1-X
A catalogue record for this book is available from the British Library

Bukowski Journal, PO Box 11271, Wood Green, London, N22 8BF, Great Britain
email: Bukzine@aol.com

Editorial

Welcome to *Bukowski Unleashed!* Bukowski Journal Vol:#1

The Journal picks up where *Bukowski Zine #4* left off, but now being in book format - I couldn't really call it a Zine any more. There where times ("I guess you knew") I had to think long and hard about wether to continue with *Bukowski Zine* but then, Inspired by David Kerekes new format *Headpress Journal,* plus my receiving more submissions via the Internet - I suddenly saw the potential to take things in. Don't worry, I'll still be schlepping a fat-bastard-bag around London via the bus & tube (Travel Card Distribution inc) but at least spotty 17 year old assistants will look more kindly on taking a book than a tatty Zine from a grown man's hand.

If you enjoy the Bukowski Journal and want to contribute to Volume #2 - feel free! Bukowski related essays, articles, reviews & art are always welcome but **please avoid** sending Bukowski influenced poetry and stories. (Arrgh!)
Reviews of other things un-Bukowski are also welcome (See the reviews section for ideas)
E-mail or write (SAE) to get a **free Bukowski check list** every month. It lists the latest Bukowski Books, Video's, Tapes, CD's available or to be released! (*Publishers! Please send us anything Bukowski related for review in Bukowski journal #2)

Last thing, while surfing the web - don't forget to check out the *'Cool Contacts'* section at the back, Believe me , there's some great www sites to visit when your between Kleenex...

Rikki Hollywood: Bukzine@aol.com

"Remember! Perception is intentional"

...Clive Saunders, by the way, is from your country...a theatre director and screenwriter. "Love For $17.50" is his first film directorial effort. He was originally lined up in partnership with Susan Rogers to produce and write the screenplay version.... they had another director attached (with whom will remain nameless)....that previous director had a film and tv background in production...but he did not have a handle on the storyline whatsoever...As a cinematographer my job is to help visually interpret that vision...and the first director had none...which was making my and the Susan Rogers job difficult. Clive on the other hand had produced and directed theatrical versions of Bukowski's work for over 8 years and was exceptionally well versed with insights to Bukowski's vision.....plus he was also in constant contact with Linda Bukowski. When Clive arrived last summer to do the rewrites of the script it was determined between Susan Rogers, myself and Clive (remember he was also one of the producers) that he should direct the project......Between Susan Rogers hustle, Clives insight and my technical background in filmmaking we moved forward. This was going to be a low budget, 16mm project that was to be made with guts and determination....

Part of this production was done through an organization called "The Filmmakers Alliance"....which is specifically

designed as a hands on self help group to help those who do not have large financial backgrounds to pull off their independant films.

I as a cinematographer knew I was going to have my hands full.....I was to work with a first time director and the budget was going to be super tight....With Susan Rogers wizardry in hustle we managed to get a complete 16mm camera package from Camtec, a ten ton truck of lighting and grip equipment packed into a five ton truck, three days on a stage, two days on location and a crew of over thirty people for free.

As you know the story of "Love For $17.50" is about a man who replaces his insane girlfreind with the perfect woman...a mannequin. Only to be busted by the real life girlfreind with explosive results.

To help the director out we actually spent one day shooting a videotape "rehearsal" of the project. This was going to help us in three ways...one: get the director use to the mechanics of filmmaking, two: get us all familiar with the story better..and three figure out roughly what kind of budget problems we were going to go through when we did the real thing. We shot that at the home of an eccentric wealthy woman in Bel Air. Very funny place, as we taped it in her "trophy room". This woman used to hunt wild animals in Africa in the 30's and 40's and we shot one of the love scenes with the Mannequin on a tiger skin rug.....tiger head included.

So the real deal was a few weeks later doing a five day shoot both on stage and on locations in various parts of Los Angeles. On stage, where they just shot the new Mod Squad tv series, we built a complete set of the apartment, art directed by Benjamin Edelberg.
Our philosophy was dark, drab and unhappy. So the sets were designed accordingly.
There was heavy communication between the director, art di-

rector and myself on the color scheme and paint colors to be used on this set. The closet was probably the most fun...as "Stella" the mannequin, was going to be living in it for a number of scenes. Benjamin designed a "perspective" closet....very wide at the top and very narrow on the bottom....and we only lit it with one light bulb! We knew this room of all others was pretty much what the story was all about..a place to put "things away", to hide "things", Store them for future use.....at one's "convenience" . It's how many men treat their own wives and girlfreinds....and it's a very ungrateful place to be at.

We knew that in doing this job that many of us were going to be going through our own journeys and philosophies of life and relationships. Which made the project that much more intensive. And believe me it was an intensive journey.

When we shot the "rape" scene..the first time Robert actually has sex with his new found partner we realized last minute that we were shooting too many of the sexual scenes in the living room....I suggested that we do the rape scene in the kitchen as that was a much colder environment which reflected the mood of the action. Clive Saunders agreed and that scene is now extremely powerful. Plus we did it handheld to give it a raw edge to it. The crew I think had a hard time watching it too. Even though we were working with a mannequin ...she was still a major character ...and at times we treated her as if she was a real human being....just as the actor did.

We actually had four mannequins...one was a "stand in" one. (the stand in was an old storefront peice and it got pretty banged up when we did the video tape rehearsal with it) And the other three were especially made for us...We requested three because we knew one of them was going to get destroyed and it was also easier to have wardrobe and hair changes made by having her ready made. One nice thing about a mannequin is that you didn't have to feed her, didn't have to wait for

South of the North Pole Presents

Scenes from the Buried Life

By
CHARLES BUKOWSKI

adapted from his book South of No North
(courtesy of Black Sparrow Press)
by Justin Rosenholtz and Clive Saunders

Directed by Clare Walters

April 6th - 24th (Not Mondays) • Starts
£5.00 £3.50 Concessions

Kings Road • Chelsea • London SW3 5UZ • Te

her..and didn't have to deal with an attitude problem. Hmmmmm I'm catching myself here...and I think you know why....

You may want to talk to Susan and Clive about who and where the mannequins came from....but I know that they got it from a high end place and we specifically got a mannequin that leaned more towards the voluptous side. There is a whole world in the people who are in the business of manufacturing mannequins...I remember taking a look at the catalogue for them ...and it was like looking a fashion magazine....it was a bit unsettling. Lifeless bodies for sale.

One note...the main actor who played "Robert" (Mickey Swenson),approached his role with method acting. I believe he actually had one of the mannequins live with him for about a month...at one point he took it with him to his daughters birthday party!

Anyway....I think once this project come out I don't think the audience will be disapointed....we tried to keep to the heart of the story line as much as we could in the realms of the budget that we had to work with and we have ,I think, quite a powerful little story about the dark inner soul of Los Angles and of human beings in general.

I could write more...and i hope this helps you out...if you want more info..please feel free to give me a call or on the net..and by all means give the director and the producer a ring...this is just as much their "baby" as mine..."what bastard son we have brought forth to teach the world a lesson"....

    Sincerely
    Luc G. Nicknair
    Cinematographer

A Drunken Sage?

by A. Monk

Bukowski often referred to moments when the writing was going well and he was hitting his stride on the type writer or computer as "Magic" and, as with every age, be it from an east or west culture, there has been various accounts of 'Magic' or 'Higher consciousness' or ' mystical and super normal experiences' etc, all which describe transporting and rapturous moments. Saint Paul called it "the peace passeth understanding." in Zen the term used for it is "Satori" or "Kensho"; in Yoga, "Samadhi" or "Moksha"; in Taoism, "the Absolute Tao"; and the Sufis speak of "Fana." G.I. Gurdjieff called it "objective consciousness"; the Quakers call it "the Inner Light"; Catholicism speaks of the "unio mystica." but what ever name it's given, there is no divergence in the description of it's effective power: it can be, and is, studied with total life- absorption by eminent scholars, as well as those untold millions of seekers who aspire to know it for themselves; Bukowski would often find it pouring out of him into words as he hammered away at the page. He drank and 'would just let it come' some nights it came easier than others but whatever came out, Bukowski would be trying to *see* something. The truth or at least how he saw it from his angle in *that* moment, be it a fist thrown at him unannounced to a land lady's footsteps getting heavier the more money owed.

But then again perhaps truth isn't a good enough word. After all truth is subjective and who's rules are we playing by anyway? You have to know all that before you can start going out saying what's right and wrong. Bukowski preferred to play it by his own instinct. Gut feeling stuff that didn't let his old man grind him down. And this is why the writing is so good and still stands up today. It's not contrived and to a formula or style that I feel limits writers like *Kerouac, *Ginsberg, *Miller, *Burroughs etc. You can kind of tell that Bukowski has gone into things in his life with his mind open but perhaps you might say he has gone into them expecting the worst and through this attitude has brought the crap on himself. Yet he wasn't prepared to buckle and become normal submissive 'Joe Public' in the work place and do what he's told. Well he was, and he wasn't. He did do over a decade at the post office sorting and delivering letters in a mind numbingly boring job but again, this is just an individuals perception. (Have you put in over ten years where you worked?!) There are hundreds of ways that you can argue for and against someone when you want to put a point across. I know Bukowski was a drunken, womanising, gambling, bar fighting slob but to me that isn't the point. I like him because he was genuine. Pure? Well the word pure comes across to me again like the word truth, it's a bit rigid.

The new age man talks about purity; The truth is the essence of purity. Purity of motive and purity of living. To bring the brain under the complete control of the will instead of at the mercy of outside influences. By carefully planned exercises he trains his mental equipment in much the same way as a dancer trains her muscles. The dancer gains complete control of her body at the cost of tremendous work and sacrifice. The sage, for about the same cost of effort, gains complete control of the mind.

Now that's all well and good getting the mind to be totally pure and totally honest to the will but how can we trust the will? Think on this: if we have started reading these all Zen and New Age books on controlling our minds and calming it down through meditation and the like...what made us reach for the books in the first place? Answer: Our will. The very thing we're now going to say we're going to control. Don't kid yourself. You will always be one step ahead of yourself. Your thought comes first. All your analysing and views have to come second.

A. Monk (Hermit.com)

*At the time of writing this article I really didn't have time for these writers, however since reading **'Naked Angels'** by John Tytell (Grove press) I've revised my opinion. I still don't like their writing much but I can now appreciate what 'mind-state' they were trying to achieve with their writing style.

STEAL THIS BOOK NOW!

The literary reputations of Charles Bukowski and Jack Kerouac are not in danger of falling into obscurity. Just ask the security guards at your local bookstore...

by Alexander Goins (ssutter@mindspring.com)

As I'm browsing through the aisles of my local independent bookstore in San Francisco one night, commotion breaks out at the front door. An employee blocks one of the customers as he's walking out and accuses him of trying to steal a book. The employee sticks his hand straight out toward the customer like he's directing traffic, and their voices start to rise. The customer, about 20 years old, tells the employee right to his face that he's full of shit and he better get the hell out of the way. There's some Sumo-style pushing and shoving, and eventually the customer breaks free and darts out, but not before the employee grabs his jacket and a book falls out onto the floor. The customer runs down the street into the night without looking back. The book on the floor is Pulp by Charles Bukowski.

With biographies and articles and classes and reading groups and new editions of their books springing up all the time, the literary reputations of Charles Bukowski and Jack Kerouac are not in danger of falling into obscurity. Many readers also tend to harbor an indulgent nostalgia for whatever was happening a generation or two ago, the same way that films often relive the past (American Graffiti and more recently, Pulp Fiction with its '70s nostalgia), and this may find its literary equivalent in Bukowski and Kerouac. Their books are enthusiastically passed along from reader to reader, creating a sort of chain-letter effect. And some literature lovers who have never read a word of either American bard get irreversibly hooked on one or both of the writers' sensibilities, especially the younger readers who identify with the out-and-out hedonism and down-and-out poverty that the two often write about. Since the death of the hard-drinking, hard-smoking Bukowski in 1994 and the emergence of Kerouac as the king of, or at least the prince of, the so-called Beat Generation (Ginsberg will always be the queen), book theft is one unorthodox manner in which their reputations are thriving -- especially among bookstore denizens, owners and employees.

The people who are perhaps the most familiar with this phenomenon are the security guards who work in the superstores such as Barnes & Noble and Borders. Sometimes wearing uniforms and sometimes in street clothes, they have a good feel for what customers most often try to lift from the shelves and speed-walk out the door with. "You get to know who's going to try to pull something off," says Jason Williams, an incognito security guard for Borders in San Diego. "They usually have a look about them, and their body language gives something away. I can't really name what it is, but I know it when I see it."

When I ask him about the literature/fiction section, he lowers his head and without thinking about it for too long says, "It's mostly Bukowski and Kerouac. You can tell when someone's

CHARLES BUKOWSKI

after those two. They have a look about them. Young usually. And maybe a little more raggedy than the others in the section. There are customers who steal other books from that section, but it seems like those two are constant. Sometimes we get one person who gets hooked on one writer, like Nabokov or someone like that, and we get wise to it and catch them and then Nabokov's books stop disappearing. But with those other two, it seems like there's always someone new trying to get at them. Maybe they're just hitching across the country stealing books; I'm not sure."

Most bookstore managers and owners agree that the No. 1 motivation for book theft is the possibility of reselling the books for cold hard cash. Because of this, expensive books such as art books and coffee table books are hot targets because of their high resale values, and best sellers are also popular targets because they are in high demand and can be resold easily. But with Bukowski and Kerouac, most managers and owners have an intuition (based upon the appearance of the thieves) that they actually steal the books to read them rather than resell them.

Ken Samuels, an employee at Browser Books in San Francisco, describes the typical readers of Bukowski and Kerouac he's encountered at the store. "Bukowski readers tend to be like a character you would find in a Bukowski book. They're usually poor and maybe even alcoholics. Down and outs. Kerouac readers are usually young, urban hipster types."

At this small, independent bookstore, they try to keep just one title on the shelf at a time rather than multiple copies of the same book, and Samuels says that Bukowski and

Kerouac books disappear more often than other books in the literature section. Without the luxury of being able to hire their own security guards, employees of smaller bookstores also notice customers who stand in the B and K sections of the literature wall and make furtive glances to see if anyone's watching them browse.

A Clean Well-Lighted Place for Books in San Francisco has noticed the problem and has taken possibly the most radical step to alleviate it. When browsing the shelves of the literature wall, customers come to the B section where Bukowski's books would normally be, and instead of his books, there is a cardboard box about the size of a large novel on which is written in black pen that customers interested in looking through Bukowski's books should proceed to the front counter to ask for "assistance." The same type of box with the same type of note is placed in the spot where Kerouac's books would normally be. Directly behind the front counter is a glass case with some of the more expensive art books on the top shelves, and then down below are all of Bukowski's and Kerouac's books behind the case's glass doors.

One can't help but think that with their bohemian lives and free-spirited poverty, both of the American bards would be smirking if they knew about what was happening with their books and their reputations.

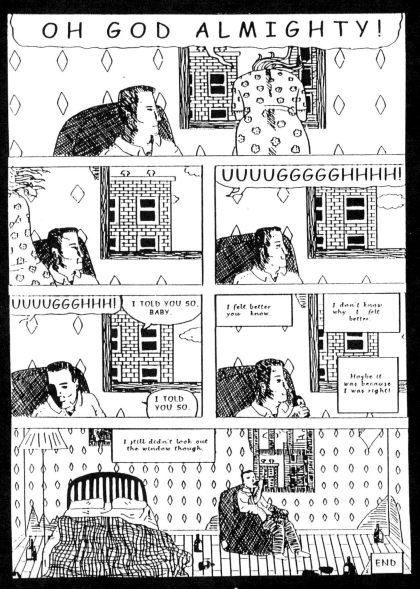

Love Is A Dog From Hell

by michael d. meloan

THE INVITATION TO A PRIVATE SCREENING and *apres* party came in the mail, then a phone call from Linda Bukowski.
"You and Cathy are the only non-Hollywood people we're inviting," she said.
Hot-Cha, I thought. I was still doing my rock band, The Dead Beats, and I thought I could bring along some cassettes, and shake hands with the tape in my palm.
"My God," Cathy said, "You're not really going to pull a stunt like that, are you? Don't you have any self respect?"
I went off to my room to dupe some tapes.
When the big night came, I was ready to rock. My sport coat was bulging with cassettes and write-ups on the band. We went early and sat in the middle of the theater reading a bio on the young Belgian director who had made a film based on Hank's short stories. Hank and Linda were nowhere to be seen, but I spotted Ginger from *Gilligan's Island*. She was wearing a skin tight black leather mini-skirt and bustier top. She looked great, her wig had been tightened up, same day-glo copper hair—time had stood still.
Suddenly a murmur came over the crowd. Hank and Linda

Charles Bukowski

had just arrived with Sean and Madonna in tow. Madonna was wearing a black velvet Gaucho outfit with a little black hat rimmed with dangling "beaner balls." Sean and Madonna both looked tiny. I had heard so much about how bad he was, and I was surprised at his size. He looked pissed-off all the time. His mouth was a tight little slit. They sat in the back in an area that had been roped off with a large red velvet sausage. I saw Hank pull out a polished chrome hip flask and take a drink, then he tried to pass it to Madonna. She held up her hand and wrinkled her nose.
"Love is a Dog from Hell" was a surprisingly good film. It was Hank's work crossed with the sensibilities of a moody European, and it worked. Everyone filed out, and we watched Hank and Linda and Sean and Madonna get into her white Cadillac stretch limo. I was right next to Ginger again, and I could smell the perfume in her hair, and see her up close. I had jerked off to her many times in my dorm room at USC, and here I was standing right next to her. She had incredibly great legs for an older broad.
We arrived at Helena's on the edge of Koreatown. It was a ramshackle dive in a shitty neighborhood just west of the civic center. There were armies of car park valets ready to take on the endless stream of Benzes, BMWs and limos. Linda said, "Helena's is Hollywood's hippest club." The owner was Jack Nicholson's long-time housekeeper. He had bankrolled the whole deal, and installed his friends as regulars, which instantly put the place on the map. If you had targeted the building with a Cruise missile on a Saturday night, 80% of young Hollywood would have been wiped off the map.
As the party got going, I went into the bathroom. While I was standing at the urinal, Sean walked up and took the next position. I glanced over to see what he had in his pants, and he looked back at me with slitted eyes full of fury. I thought about trying to give him a cassette, but decided that might not be a good idea. As I was washing my hands, he glanced at me in the mirror. His eyes looked like

granite. He was like a beaker of nitro-glycerine. If you jiggled the container, the whole place would be blown to smithereens.

Inside Helena's was O. K., but no great shakes. The tables were like picnic benches. Two people got up from a slot across from Hank and Linda, Cathy and I sat down. Linda and Hank were talking to Gisela Getty, the German wife of J. Paul Getty III. He was the guy who had his ear cut off by Italian mobsters when the old man (J. Paul Getty I) wouldn't cough up one red cent to get his grandson off the meat hook. They cut off his ear and sent it to the family—but still no dice. Finally they let him go. J. Paul spent the next 10 years partying with this beautiful German and her identical twin sister. He was living with them both as wives. I read that they all three slept in the same bed, but he was legally married only to Gisela. After an all night blowout on coke, heroin and booze, he had a massive cerebral stroke and ended up deaf, dumb and blind. He needed round the clock nurses, so Gisela left to become a "reporter." She was trying to report on Hank.

We sat down, and I arched my back and smiled at Gisela. A candle was flickering between us—she looked very beautiful. I watched the light dance on her face and hair. She leaned over and whispered something to Linda.

"Oh no!" Linda said, "Not at all."
"What did she say?" I asked Linda.
"She said that you seem like a big phony," Linda said.

My mouth dropped open. I thought she and I had something going. I was even thinking of giving her a cassette. I got up and moved around to Hank's end of the table, leaving my wife with Gisela and Linda. Hank was taking long drinks of red wine and talking to the Belgian film director, who looked young enough to be in high school. Hank was very friendly to him.

"I liked it kid," he said. "In fact, I think it's better than 'Barfly'..." ("Barfly" hadn't been released, but was already in the can.)

Linda heard this comment, and turned her head, "Oh, no! It's just different. Don't say things like that, Papa!"

Hank growled slightly and took another drink. Then he introduced me to the director, and we all drank expensive Merlot together. Suddenly I looked up, and the black Gaucho hat with dangling balls was hovering above. The translucent white face of Madonna was looking down on me. She was holding a cigarette between two fingers, up level with her ear. Sean walked up from behind. The people sitting right next to Hank got up and left on cue. As if a dangerous gunfighter had just come into the saloon, and the seas began to part. Madonna sat down next to the director, right across from me, and Sean sat on Hank's other side. I heard Sean telling Hank that he'd like to option "Women" for screen rights. Hank perked up a little. I looked straight across the table at those dangling balls. They were moving all the time. I felt my coat pocket—plenty of tapes.

"Hi," I finally said to her. "How ya doin'?"

She just looked into my eyes with an icy stare, took a deep drag from her cigarette, and blew the smoke right into my face. She continued to stare, so I finally got up to go to the bathroom. On the way I ran into Billy Idol.

"Hi. How ya' doin'?" I said again.
"How YOU doin'?" he asked back.
"I'm doing O.K. I'd be doing better though, if I had a recording contract."
"Is that right? Wodda you do?" he asked.
"I'm a rock singer?"
"Is that right? Why don't you sing something for us right now," he said.

Michael Monfort

I had won a $100 lip-synching contest in a nightclub down in Sarasota, Florida doing "Break on Through" by the Doors, so I thought I'd try that. I started in, *"You know the day destroys the night..."* And I felt like I was doing O. K. At one point I looked over at the Bukowski table—Linda and Cathy were shooting me daggers. I did a few more verses and quit. Billy took a drink from a highball glass.

"Not bad, not bad," he said.

The young blond with him looked like she was getting bored, so I figured I'd better cut to the chase.

"Well, it's been good meeting you," I said, reaching out to shake his hand. He extended his hand, and looked very surprised when he felt the tape. He opened his hand and took a look at the cassette, just as I turned and headed to the men's room. I looked over my shoulder just before going in, and saw him toss the tape into the trash can next to the bar. On the way out of the bathroom, a dark haired middle aged woman who looked like a Gypsy came up to me.

"Hello. I'm Helena. And you are?"

"I'm Ralph Pontoon," I told her.

"Who invited you tonight?" she asked.

"Bukowski," I said.

She frowned, "Do you mind if we go over and verify that Mr. Bukowski knows you.?"

"Yeah, that's O. K." I said.

The crowd had started to thin out. When we got back to the long table, Sean and Madonna were gone.

Only Linda, Hank, Cathy, Gisela, and the Belgian Director were left.

"Mr. Bukowski, do you mind my asking if you know this man?"

I felt like I was being busted after the bell rang in junior high, and now I was going to the principal's office.

"I know the fuck," said Hank. "I'll take care of him, leave him with me."

"Thanks," I said, after she left.

"Listen kid, you've got something, I can see it. But you need to stop bullshitting yourself. Chasing all this glamour and pussy is a big fucking waste of time. Take it from me...a 67 year old man." He started laughing, and looked at me with slitty eyes and a cracked smile. Then he poured me another big glass of Merlot.

"I propose a toast," he said, while we all raised our glasses.

"To the night when Meloan finally gets real. Whenever that will be."

I guess it's high time I checked out **CrimeTime** Magazine and get me some **Ed Bunker** books from **No Exit Press!**

Www.noexit.co.uk
Www.crimetime.co.uk

SAMUEL BECKETT
BECKETT SHORTS - Special New Editions
1. Texts For Nothing
2. Dramatic Works
3. All Strange Away
4. Worstward Ho
5. Six Residua
6. For To End Yet Again
7. The Old Tune
8. First Love
9. As The Story Was Told
10. Three Novellas
11. Stirrings Still
12. Selected Poems

The Major Works Boxed Set £30

CALDER PUBLICATIONS

Introduction to Neil Schiller's essay

'I kept on walking around the big room, pulling the books off the shelves, reading a few lines, a few pages, then putting them back.
Then one day I pulled a book down and opened it, and there it was.'

(Bukowski – Introduction to John Fante's 'Ask the Dust', 1979)

Perhaps boredom is the key to it all. Just as he discovered John Fante, so I first stumbled across Bukowski. Wandering aimlessly around a bookstore in Liverpool, picking things up and reading the first couple of sentences and putting them all back because they seemed shite. And then I saw a copy of 'Notes of a Dirty Old Man' laid out on a table and I picked it up because I liked the way it looked and I opened it up because the back read like a challenge: go on, hate this writer, plenty of people do already. I remember being struck by the chaotic style of writing and the brutal honesty in a lot of the essays - Bukowski telling it like it is - and how close he was getting to the core of it all. And this great story where a guy with wings joins a losing baseball team and gets screwed over by the gambling commission, which just seemed like such a cool allegory and yet managed to steer clear of the usual pretentiousness in which most allegories live. I didn't realise at the time that the excerpts here were gleaned from a newspaper column Bukowski wrote in the sixties, but together they just made this fantastic, whirling collage of an American society crumbling beneath greed and commercialism and hypocrisy. Ultimately, I suppose I did it the same way round as the original readers: the newspaper columns first, then the novels and the short stories and the poetry. It's probably the best way to get a feel for what he's on about. And if he's on about boredom, if he's as interested in chaos and emptiness and meaninglessness as I think he is, then it's pretty apt that I started with some vague interest in the cover of a book, and ended with this notion of Bukowski as a genius because he isn't scared to tell us what we already know: it's all a load of bollocks.

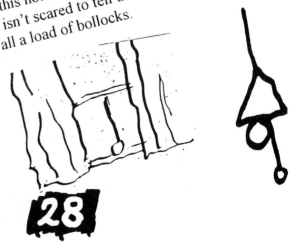

Social Mechanics and American morality: the meanings of nothingness in the prose and poetry of Charles Bukowski

by Neil Schiller

Social Mechanics and American morality: the meanings of nothingness in the prose and poetry of Charles Bukowski

by Neil Schiller
(neil.schiller@virgin.net)

> We have wasted history like a bunch of drunks shooting dice back in the men's crapper.

Central to Bukowski's vision of contemporary American society is the notion of failure, the inability of human effort to achieve anything that is worth achieving. Governments fail, revolutions fail, writing fails, and there are two basic reasons for this. The first seems to be a prevalent lack of imagination, a basic fundamental limitation of the species which curbs the reorganisation of society into something other than that which it has defaulted to be: a complex system of coercion and oppression geared towards the

retention of power for its own sake. The second is that every effort of reimagination, every proposal of restructuring is based upon an assumption of meaning. Every life must have a purpose: the accumulation of property; the trappings of personal success; the tangible essence of liberty and freedom. And each of these is bullshit. Each one is an artificial goal set by society itself to fill the void of existence, to satiate the masses and ensure economic prosperity for the few. Bukowski's America, then, is one of innate chaos and meaninglessness, anarchy masked by lies and framed by oppression. The symbols of the State and the Corporation are deliberately constructed to intimidate citizens and workers alike; to hold out vague promises of achievement and belonging while, at the same time, instilling a sense of fear in their subjects, fear of failing to live up to the requirements set. The figures of the Foreman and the Father appear constantly in Bukowski's prose and poetry as the human faces of an invisible and menacing system of authority, against which and against who no rebellion ever really succeeds. And it is not simple oppression either, but rather a subtle and tangled web of psychological suggestion and counter perception, in the workplace, in the home, in the newspapers, at the racetrack. Bukowski's characters are constantly being manipulated and herded into ideological positions and attitudes intended to keep them from realising their lack of freedom: the Post Office, for instance, attempts to regulate both the employed mind and the private one, prescribing ethical codes of conduct expected outside of working hours. A vast undercurrent of futility bubbles away underneath the surface of American society and the concealing of this void, the occasional outburst of this chaos, is fundamental to Bukowski's reading of the everyday in American life. So too is the writer's appreciation of a complex and oppressive social mechanism holding this chaos together, an appreciation which leads ultimately to an examination and a reassessment of the common precepts (law, liberty, morality) which support the existing social structure.

It is perhaps in the writing that details his period of employment at the Post Office and the years immediately preceding this that Bukowski best depicts the despotic nature of the Corporation, the employer, and its efforts to govern the lives of its workers out of its own self-interest. The novel *Post Office*, for example, begins with a copy of an actual memo distributed to all members of staff declaring that "postal personnel are expected to maintain the highest moral principles". The reason given for this is that the postal workers are the most public face of the federal government and as such need to give a good impression of this institution. This may or may not be a valid reason for an infringement upon personal liberty, but it becomes a point of interest when compared to a remark made by the novel's hero Chinaski a few pages later:

What did the Postal Manual say? Where was it? I had never known anybody who had seen one.

Whereas the postal authority can distribute a vaguely worded directive to act in a moral manner, it chooses to refrain from elaborating upon this, from elaborating on other standard procedures, and from clarifying workers' rights in a handbook. In light of this, the memo then becomes a vague threat, an assertion of power that draws its strength from misinterpretation. By refraining from elaboration, the authority ensures that it alone has access to definitions of what its directives might mean, effectively empowering itself against its subjects, free to use its decrees against them in whichever way it sees fit. And this is not the only method that the post office is seen to embrace in order to coerce its employees into modes of behaviour and productivity beneficial to itself. At one point in the novel, a series of posters turn up around the offices in an attempt to whip up patriotism in the workers:

> EACH EXTRA LETTER YOU STICK BEYOND DUTY HELPS DEFEAT THE RUSSIANS.

After working for weeks without any days off, Chinaski is looking forward to four days in lieu away from his job, but just as he is about to leave, the message comes over the staff intercom: "YOUR FOUR DAYS OFF HAVE BEEN CANCELLED". It is clear from these instances that there is no tactic left untried by the authority in question in its attempt to psychologically manage and manipulate its workers. If it cannot turn them into a "brainwash job" by blitzing them with tired notions of patriotic guilt, then it seeks to demoralise them through a deliberate policy of overwork, disarming and disorientating its workforce with immediate, unexpected and absolute decisions.

Chinaski's relationship with this power structure is a complex one, primarily because he is aware of the rules and methods of power, and yet is a part of the system himself and unable to really influence it in any way. Indeed, his very first day as a clerk at the post office sets the tone for things to come. As he sits filling a tray with mail, he is told along with the other new clerks that they have to complete their duties in a specified time frame. Immediately, those around him begin to pack trays as quickly as they can, "arms...flying" with "fear of failure", while he takes his time, figuring right away that the target is unrealistic. And it pays off: he is so far behind the others that the supervisor presumes he is in fact on his second tray and is "making production", to which Chinaski's response is to "slow...down a little more". In effect, he has already found a way to beat the system, partly

by bluffing and using its own rules against itself, and partly by refusing to follow the guidelines set for him. After all, as Chinaski observes, it is the workers themselves who make the ridiculous deadlines and methods of manipulation possible "by obeying...impossible orders". What is ironic, however, is precisely the way in which Chinaski derides his co-workers for allowing their jobs to take over their lives and their individuality, and yet becomes himself ensnared in precisely the same manner. In *Factotum*, for instance, he criticises his father for having "no other subject except the job" in any of his thoughts or conversations. In *Post Office* he observes the way in which G.G. "the dedicated man" is "knifed across the throat over a handful of circs from a local market". He criticises all this, expresses disgust over the way these people allow themselves to be taken over, and yet when caught in a flood while collecting the post, he expresses joy at "outwitt[ing] adversity, that Jonstone up there in the sky". Unknowingly, he has just done exactly what those others have done: defined an instance in his life, defined himself, in the narrow terms of reference of his job. He has not just defeated God, he has not just defeated chance or luck or even the Devil. He has defeated his supervisor; he has defeated his supervisor in his many forms, this time Fate. The inversion is telling. Chinaski is not looking down on his superior in work from above, comparing him to a deity, to a higher malevolent power. He is looking up at that higher power through his supervisor and constructing the larger framework in the language and images of the smaller one. In effect, despite all his observations and all his knowledge, Chinaski is revealed politically as merely another worker, trapped in the same nets of frailty and powerlessness as everyone else. He is the "shipping clerk, receiving clerk, stock boy" who does not "know how to do anything"; the subjective narrator speaking from within his bleak and hopeless world; the authoritative and earnest voice of truth made more powerful by his human fallibility and shared weaknesses.

Outside of the Post Office, the tactics of oppression are slightly more subtle but no less effective. In the short story "The Stupid Christs", for example, Bukowski depicts the average working class American family man as someone who reluctantly gives "half their salar(y)...to state and federal taxes" but then waste the rest on "new cars, color tv, stupid wives and four or five different types of insurance". In essence, the dream of material wealth is coupled with a paranoid fear of losing what things an individual has accumulated to ensure they continue working, in thrall of money, ultimately benefiting the employer. The trick is not only in the incentive, but in making the worker believe he is reaping the rewards of his own labour. "You never had it so good" is a line Bukowski's heroes (Chinaski and the assorted short story protagonists) hear from their co-workers in every job, "no matter how shitty" the work involved is or how poorly paid the workers are. Indeed, such is the extent of this narrow vision in the working class that Bukowski has to look far afield for examples of success against the system. In this case it is Mexico, a country "close enough to the U.S. to speak the language and know its corruption", and yet far enough away to look objectively on ways in which it can gain from American society. He compares it to "a suckerfish attached to the belly of a shark", evidently admiring the manner in which it draws wealth away from its neighbour through the allurement of gambling and drink. So there is some hope against the absolute power of the predominant American ideology of material success and acquisition, unearthed here in an ability to play against the game of acquiring wealth with its own rules. It is almost like winning the occasional battle in a war you are doomed to lose, because the individual must operate within a structure, must exist within a wider frame of existence. He might manage to manipulate this from time to time, they might learn to live in a manner which is beneficial to themselves, but they only do so in the terms of the system. Whether oppressed by, enlightened by, or reactive to ideology, you nevertheless remain defined by its rules of being:

We can choose between Nixon and Humphrey and
Christ and be fucked anyway we turn.

In a sense, there is in Bukowski's work a fourth option:
neither Nixon, Humphrey nor Christ, but Bukowski. He is
perpetually aware of the terms of existence, he is aware of
his place within this greater frame of being, and he trusts
none of it, is sceptical about all of it, relies on his own instincts and nothing else. Which is akin to the suckerfish and
the shark: something which exists primarily in opposition to
something other; is ironically defined by a contrary force to
which it owes the debt of its evolution.

Perhaps the best example of this ironic, impotent liberation
can be found in Bukowski's depiction of the racetrack. In
"Goodbye Watson", for example, the racetrack is initially
depicted as something representational of the American
dream of wealth. It promises a real chance at financial success and offers the individual some form of personal achievement, picking the winners and beating the betting system.
And yet, "the racetrack [too] is just another JOB finally",
another element in the system of control that keeps the
smitten and manipulated hoards in a docile state, "getting
nowhere, waiting on Papa Death, getting [their] mind(s)
kicked to hell and [their] spirit(s) kicked to hell". Again,
Bukowski is no exception. He knows the rules of the track
and he knows the tricks and methods used by race organisers
to fleece money from the gamblers, and yet he is again
subject to these tricks himself, explaining in depth why "One-
Eyed Jack" is a terrible horse, a sucker's bet, and yet admitting to having bet on it himself. Because of this, however, the
track for Bukowski is a means of strengthening himself
against the trails of existence, of reaffirming his knowledge

of the structure of society and helping him plan his means of resistance. Just as the Bullfights were for Hemingway "a drawingboard of everything", the place "were everything attached to everything", so too for Bukowski is the racetrack a microcosm of the world he inhabits, the American social construct he exists within:

> The racetrack tells me quickly where I am weak and where I am strong.

There is an incident depicted in *Notes of a Dirty Old Man* which pins down several aspects of Bukowski's vision of American society in precisely this hopeful/hopeless manner. It begins with the author musing on precisely why the racetrack is so perpetually crowded when basically, people are "driven screwy by the turn of the bolt" here just as they are at work, at home, everywhere else. Sure, there is a chance of winning, but this is so slight and the races are so rigged that any gain is ultimately outweighed by the losses. Indeed, the only answer Bukowski can arrive at is that "some of us finally love our tormentors", that the populace becomes so accustomed to being manipulated and oppressed that it seems normal, the "logical lines of torture" providing a sort of ideological comfort:

> We build our own racks and scream when our genitals are torn off.

Except, of course, that we do not always scream, sometimes we sigh instead. What then happens is that a horse which seems a very good bet (likely to win and set at fairly high odds) is shown on the tote board to be suddenly dropping in price. It wins the race, but the payout advised is far below what it should be. Basically, the bookmakers involved have made some sort of initial mistake and, in order to minimise their losses, decide to cheat the betting crowd, a tactic which results in chaos. Several people storm onto the track and begin shouting to the rest of the crowd to stop betting, to repay the greed and immorality of the gambling commission by cutting off their income, and, of course, it does not work. The gamblers cannot stop gambling, they are "hooked, bleeding, gotten forever". "The mob [has] been knifed, again", and they are only too aware of this, but instead of reacting, they submit. Because that is easier; because that is what they are used to; because they do not want to rebel against something they have been taught to love, no matter that it is only available in the terms of authority. Which is exactly Bukowski's point. Revolt is futile because it is not simply a case of the popular voice against the oppressor. The modes of control and manipulation are infinitely more complex than this. Revolt against the oppressor is a revolt against the self, is a turning against several fundamental principles of existence for an individual within society. We are not merely physically oppressed by various facets of authority, but also taught to like the way things are. Ideology is the killer because it traps the individual in singular notions of how and why and breeds from these a familiarity with the way things should be. Revolt is futile because the bigger picture is at once too big to tackle and too personally compact to shake, which leaves Bukowski trapped in a kind of social stalemate:

> Christ slipped off the cross and we are now nailed to the motherfucker, black and white, white and black, completely.

It is a stalemate which permeates every facet of human existence: the factory; the state; the family. Even as a very young child, for instance, Bukowski's hero Chinaski can recall being forced by his parents to "pick [a] spoon up with [his] right hand" when he in fact wants to do so with his left. Right from the very beginning, he is pressured into conformity, made to repress his natural left-handedness because the other way of being is considered more normal. Indeed, the home of the young Chinaski is very much a microcosm of American society at large, and through the initially innocent and immature eyes of the protagonist, Bukowski is able to uncover the absolute ludicrousness of the ethical values Chinaski's parents, and thousands of other American parents, structure their lives around. They worry about "what...the neighbours think" when in fact they "never spoke to the neighbours"; they desperately want to be wealthy and so "imagine...themselves rich" rather than accept their circumstances; they remain convinced of the notion that a man is defined by what he does, what he "wants(s) to be", even when his father becomes unemployed. Indeed, so ingrained is this final precept that Chinaski's father continues to leave the house when unemployed, pretending to go to work so the neighbours will not know of his predicament. It becomes increasingly clear as the novel progresses that everything in the Chinaski household, everything of worth in the ideology of Chinaski's father, is geared around the accumulation of material wealth. At one point the young hero is chastised for his interest in classical music, and when his mother defends him by claiming he at least has an interest, his father's retort is that "he doesn't DO anything with it! He doesn't make it USEFUL!". Chinaski's father, Henry senior, is presented in *Ham on Rye* as the archetypal working class man who is hooked on the false promises of an American dream of

wealth. He even has a theory eked out which has the father buying a house and passing it on to his son, who then buys a second house, passing them both on to his son, and so on, resulting in some far off descendent in possession of considerable property and wealth. Of course, it is a ludicrous idea, but what is interesting about it is the rigid focus on property ownership as a means to prosperity. As Russell Harrison points out in his essay "Politics, Class and the Plebeian Tradition", "the dream of home ownership" is central to systems of working class oppression because it gives the individual something to lose and therefore weighs heavily on their rebellious impulses. That Chinaski's father is so enamoured of this dream places him squarely in the centre of "the whole petty-bourgeois ideological sub-ensemble", struggling to achieve out of the "economic insecurity and status anxiety" engineered to keep him that way.

In his biography of the author, *Bukowski, A Life*, Neeli Cherkovski suggests that Bukowski's "view of his father became a blueprint for his view of society", representing as he does in fictional form "the oppressive factor", the social forces "trying to press down and annihilate" individuality. It is certainly true that the ideology of Henry senior in *Ham on Rye* is one of the major influences on the conclusions Chinaski comes to about the nature of social existence and human opportunity. This process perhaps begins in earnest when the adolescent hero considers one of his father's favourite beliefs in relation to the reality of the life of his parents:

> Early to bed and early to rise, makes a man healthy, wealthy and wise.

"It hadn't done any of that for him" concludes Chinaski, who then decides that the logical path for him to follow in light of this revelation is "to reverse the process", to effectively reject everything that his father has believed in. Whether this is as crucial a juncture as Russell Harrison suggests, the "rejection of a world-view which has reduced the father to something less than human", is questionable, but Bukowski is certainly here starting to question some of the fundamental beliefs and values which underpin the American social and ethical structure. Chinaski realises that the working class individuals locked into these values and belief systems of his father are no better than a class of "peasant-servants who [have] surrendered their real lives for fractional and illusionary gains", an assertion which certainly does not contradict Harrison's claim that the notion of homeownership in America has created "a new serfdom". But to then suggest that all of Bukowski's writing contains traces of a "pre-conscious socialist impulse" seems somewhat misguided. This is not to say that Bukowski does not empathise with those losing out to the system, but he does so independent of any popular or overtly political ideologies. Indeed, in *Ham on Rye* he deliberately constructs Chinaski as a character either beyond political influence or one who is drawn into politics out of ulterior, even incidental, motives. During the late thirties he sides himself with the fascists, not "by temperament or choice" but simply because the general "anti-German prejudice" and overtly uniform liberalism of his teachers repulses him into contrariness and rebellion. Perhaps the best illustration of Chinaski's ideological perspective in this novel is the point where he proclaims himself agnostic, basically because "agnostics didn't have much to argue about". There exists in Chinaski's attitude, and in Bukowski's writing, not a pre-conscious socialism, but rather a semiconscious nihilism. Beneath religion, beneath political rhetoric, beneath the very fabric of ordinary existence, there is nothing. A vacuous chaos which consists of nothing and means nothing and can be constructed into nothing. Which is perhaps why Chinaski does not deem anything worth the effort of belief. Which is why he does not hate his father but instead experiences, while being beaten, a feeling of "being surrounded by white empty space", a barrenness of emotion which allows him to calmly conclude that this man "(is)n't much of anything".

What can then be traced in Bukowski's writing is a logical progression of thought which leads from this premise of underlying chaos framed by manipulative dreams and phantom promises, onto a critical examination of the lies, social perspectives and moral values which support the existing social structure. In the short story "A .45 to Pay the Rent", the author begins again with a description of the good old American job, this time from the point of view of an ex-convict. "There aren't any honest jobs" claims Duke, the hero of the story, only the "hype" and the "slave labor" of "shit parole". The boss can tell you to do whatever he wants, can skim off your wages and deny you anything. "One word out of you, they're on the phone", "your man stole 25 dollars". What is in essence being constructed here is a depiction of society as ridiculously twofold. Somebody somewhere decides and creates specific laws, the breaking of which results in immediate punishment, and yet immorality in a very real, ethical sense is widespread and commonplace. People are humiliated and manipulated every day, "the whole world [swims] in the shit of legal murder", and yet nothing is done about it. Things "within the law" are permissible, are not even seen to be immoral, because it is "their law", the law of the ruling classes in their many guises, created by them and for them, for their benefit and their ultimate gain. What Bukowski attempts to do in "A .45 to Pay the Rent" is to begin to address this manifestly absurd and patently hypocritical moral structure. Stealing, he claims, may well be against the law, may well be immoral, but it sure "beats working a punch-press", it sure beats killing yourself for the profit of others, making them rich while you fail to share in the rewards of your own labour. He is very careful in this story to present the main character as someone who is fundamentally a decent human being and is, apart from his criminal behaviour, otherwise ethically sound. He gives all the money he has to make his daughter happy; he asserts her independence to his wife: "she's nobody's kid", "she's her own kid"; and he displays an infinitely compassionate and unwavering honesty when faced with questions from her:

> Why do people try to hit us with their cars?
> Because they are unhappy and unhappy people like to hurt things.

Whatever Duke is, Bukowski is at pains to point out, he is not an evil or unethical man. He cares about his daughter, he cares about truthfulness and honesty, he cares about individuality. He is a rational being who makes a rational choice about the way society is structured. Thus he is left standing "outside a liquor store at Hollywood and Normandie", preparing to commit another robbery, as a symbol of revolt against the hypocritical order of American law and morality.

The concept of morality is indeed something which becomes of paramount importance to Bukowski throughout his writing. Richard Gray calls him "a frustrated moralist", struggling to come to terms with the "unfulfilled promises" of the American Dream, and there is indeed an element of truth in this. Rather than impress his own ethical ideologies on his readership, Bukowski instead tends to focus in his work much more exclusively on an examination of the ludicrousness of morality. Beneath every ethical moment of existence, behind every judgement and every ideology, there is a venomous undercurrent of subjectivity which threatens to spill out and swamp everything in uncertainty. Nothing is absolute. From a certain perspective any action, any immoral circumstance, can be justified. Perhaps the most famous instance of this can be found in *Post Office* where Chinaski delivers a letter to a single woman who is obviously rather mentally unstable. After asking for a signature for her mail, Chinaski is invited into her living room while she signs, and then is not allowed to leave. The woman blocks his exit and begins to scream at him. "THERE IS EVIL WRITTEN ALL OVER YOUR FACE". Then, when he tries to push past her, she begins to call him an "evil rapist" and what follows is essentially a scene in which Chinaski proceeds to rape the woman, doing so in a very calculating manner, fully aware of his actions and their connotations. And initially, this is rather a shocking episode, one which undermines to a great extent any empathy the reader might have with Chinaski and the suffering he endures. But what is interesting about the whole scene is the way in which Bukowski first of all goes some way towards quantifying the actions of his character and then balancing this against an innate amorality which exists at the base level of human existence. It is the woman who in fact initiates the episode by trapping Chinaski in her house, and indeed introduces the idea of rape into the exchange herself. As he leaves the house after the rape, she is depicted as "staring quietly at the ceiling", perhaps in shock but just as likely in a state of serenity which suggests the rape has not significantly disturbed her. The suggestion is indeed that she has at the least half instigated the incident, perhaps as a result of her mental instability or some other emotional need.

What is infinitely more chilling, however, is the amoral attitude of Chinaski here. The woman's seeming compliance implies that an issue such as rape is not as ethically clear cut as is usually presumed. Her serenity at the conclusion of what is usually perceived in popular ideology as an ordeal suggests morality itself is an infinitely more complex and conceptually vague notion than is generally appreciated. But what of Chinaski's actions themselves? He is called an "evil rapist" by this strange woman, and without any real hesitation he simply concludes that "she [is] right" and proceeds to live up to this judgement of him. Chinaski displays no ethical concerns or stirrings of conscience, but simply does as his imagination is prompted to do by the woman he rapes. There is not even any real motivation behind his actions, neither desire nor frustrated assertion of power, only the action itself, and what Bukowski in effect does here is to unmask morality as a frail concept, and even an artificial one. It does not exist within the moment itself, it does not exist innately within the mind of the protagonist: it is instead something which occurs (or does not occur) as an afterthought at best. It is a device created by society to govern that which is ungovernable: human impulse. At the base level of existence there are no reasons, no meanings, no motivations, only the impulsive animal actions which result from the chaotic nature of existence. Morality is a system, exactly like employment and gambling and property ownership, a system designed to contain and conceal the vacuum of meaning, the chaos which is the material fabric of existence.

Elsewhere in Bukowski's prose, the issue of morality is tackled in a variety of ways. In the collection of stories *The Most Beautiful Woman in Town*, for instance, the author uses two very different narratives in comparison to each other to undermine perceptions of morality in the reader. "The Fiend" basically centres around the sexual desires and eventual rape of a young girl by a paedophile, and Bukowski again presents the scene in an amoral manner to immediately dislocate notions of ethics in absolute terms. The young girl is presented to the reader through the perspective of the paedophile himself, "little saucy", "her tongue out", "little saucy, crawling on the grass". Rather than cast moral aspersions on his character here, Bukowski instead focuses solely on the details of the situation itself: the brooding emotions of Martin the protagonist and his intent observation of the girl's underwear. The effect of this is twofold: it serves to distance the author from the incident and in so doing creates a space within the text where morality is meaningless, where circumstances and human impulses can be examined in a more clinical manner, free from ulterior value structures. And what Bukowski uncovers in this scientific working environment is itself of great interest. At one point in the story Martin masturbates while staring at the girl from his window. As soon as he has finished doing this, the thought occurs to him that he is "free again", that the sexual thoughts and fantasies are "out of [his] mind". It is almost a purging process, the shedding of unwanted, oppressive desires in the only way possible. This suggests that Martin is another example of the disempowered individual in the work of Bukowski, this time at the mercy of chaotic and random human sexual impulses, sexuality at its most primeval. Indeed, this story serves to some extent as both an affirmation of and a contrast to the depiction of morality in the rape scene of *Post Office*. Again, it suggests that morality is a human construct, an artificial device to stem the chaos of human existence. The difference here, however, is that Bukowski is at pains to illustrate the benefits of such a construct. With morality suspended, Martin is prey to his dark and selfishly evil desires. He looks into the eyes of the girl he is raping and she is obviously frightened and agonised by the intercourse because she is so much smaller than he is, yet it is described by Bukowski as "a communication between two hells". The suffering of the child is such that it is almost unimaginable, it is beyond any real comprehension, and yet the suffering of Martin is equated to it. Despite the incredulity of the police who ultimately arrest him for his crime, despite the incredulity of the reader who is depicted the full horror of the incident, in Martin's final plea that he "couldn't help it...so help me Christ" there is conveyed the notion that morality has its purpose. Despite its artificiality, despite its employment by powers such as the state and the corporation to maintain a profitable status quo, morality nevertheless keeps the chaos of reality at bay. Morality makes sense of meaninglessness, morality shields mankind from its own worst traits, morality saves.

Immediately following "The Fiend" in this collection is another story which tackles the issue of morality from an opposite direction. In "The Murder of Ramon Vasquez", there is depicted the murder of an ageing gay film star by two young men posing as fans. In this story, the actor initially treats his two guests with great cordiality. The two young men at first seem grateful, but then start abusing their host, searching his house for money, and finally murdering him out of disgust for his sexuality. This time Bukowski makes no attempt to negate the immorality of his protagonists. It is made clear that Vasquez, as he himself summarises, has "offered [his] hospitality" and is repaid by his guests turning "brutal and unkindly". There are two aspects to the story, however, that make it of particular interest in any discussion of ethics in Bukowski's writing. The first is the way in which the two murderers try to rationalise their viciousness to themselves and to each other:

> Queers are worse than Jews. I mean Jews would rather die than give up a penny. And queers LIE.

The reiteration to themselves that Vasquez is lying justifies their brutality towards the man, but much more revealing is the application of absurd value judgements. Jews are somehow less socially acceptable than gentiles, a precept given support by the ridiculous generalisation that they are all money hoarders. Homosexuals are then less socially acceptable than Jews, and when no real reason can be found to substantiate this, the surreal claim that they are all liars is produced. Once this structure to society has been established, in however haphazard and absurd a manner, it then becomes less immoral if not patently ethical to persecute someone of 'lesser' social status. What Bukowski is in effect illustrating here is the absurd ease with which morality can be put to work in society, can be wrought and twisted to support almost any whimsical logic. Of course, the claims of the two murderers are so overtly ridiculous that the reader is not left wondering about the ultimate immorality of their actions. They label a meal they have just eaten as nothing more than "QUEER FOOD"; they mock Vasquez's sexuality, make it a reason of persecution, and then try to get him to "suck [their] cock(s)" as a tactic of intimidation. Their attempts to define what is morally acceptable behaviour are almost hilarious, and yet this brings me to the second point of interest about this story. In the collection it directly succeeds "The Fiend" and although each story originally appeared in separate publications, their ordering here seems no accident. In "The Fiend" the reader witnesses the rape and consequent murder/manslaughter of a child. In "The Murder of Ramon Vasquez" the reader witnesses the sexual intimidation and murder of an ageing gay actor. The moral indignation engendered by each of these should be of equal portion. Indeed, the transgression committed in the latter story should be consider all the more revolting as the two murderers in the latter story know precisely what they are doing, try to justify themselves even, whereas the paedophile of the former work is painstakingly depicted as powerless to control his own actions. The character of Vasquez too is elaborately painted as kind and generous whereas "little saucy" does not even have a name and is given no character development. And yet despite all these devices which would seem to make the latter misdemeanour more ethically unsound than the former, the plight of the girl still somehow seems the worse of the two. What Bukowski does here then, very cleverly, is to actually confront the reader with an acknowledgement of their own synthetic moral codes and value judgements. Just as the two murderers of Ramon Vasquez applied ultimately vague and intangible reasoning behind their moral justifications, so too does the reader arrive at ethical conclusions based on something other than clear and concise logic. Two people are sexually abused, two people are murdered, and yet the sin against the young child is greater than the sin against the middle aged queer.

The primary impulse of Bukowski's writing then, it seems, is reactive in nature, is concerned primarily with the deconstruction of man-made precepts that have passed somehow into absolute belief and acceptance. Nobody is free from these ideological traps, not the author's characters, not the author himself, not the reader. In light of this, it becomes somewhat difficult to understand fully the label attached to Bukowski by the New York Times upon his death of "descendant of the Romantic Visionaries". It is true that Bukowski "hinge(s) philosophical and meditative writings on things discernible in the real world", it is true that he determines the lives of the lower, working classes as aesthetic a subject as any other. Whereas the Romantic poets base their musings upon an innate faith in the ability of humanity to transcend its earthly traits and failings, Bukowski's writing does not seem to hold this hope. For him, the world is not one of ultimate reason and logic, but one of fundamental emptiness, void of reason, void of meaning, void of hope. Yet even pessimism is not an absolute in Bukowski's work. There are instances, particularly in his poetry, of hope in its rawest form: isolated moments in time where the very lack of meaning to things becomes the point and the poignancy and the very beauty of existence:

> ...it's dark in there like the inside of a glove
> and some of the patrons speak to each other,
> only their voices are broken and scratched and they speak
> of simple things

The poem "small cafe" deals with just such an instant of time, one fragmentary moment that unfurls in a forgotten corner of the world, and what Bukowski seems to be emphasising in the opening here is precisely the lower class aesthetic which would serve to relate his writing to that of the Romantics. The metaphor of the glove used to connote the gloom inside the cafe is a distinctly domestic one, which serves to immediately stress the lack of grandeur in the scene; a lack of grandeur then further emphasised by the flawed, human quality of the cracked voices and the uncomplicated, unsophisticated "simple things" said. The cafe is very much a typical location in the world of Bukowski: unimportant, shabby, imperfect. Much more interesting than the physical features he assures the reader of, however, are the emotions and intellectual meaning which he asserts are not present. There is "no sadness" in any of the patrons, "no rancour" either; the "young Mexican fry cook" loves "the old waitress" simply "because [he] can't help it". The waitress herself is described as *"sans everything"*, almost inhuman in her freedom from emotional ties and intellectual burdens, even ethical concerns; and yet, at the same time, she is all the more human for existing in a world where none of these things really matter because beneath them all is only the slowly turning fan with its bent blades or the old fashioned cash register; beneath them all is only the physical fabric of a reality which exists in spite of why or how. This in fact is the nature of Bukowski's faith in existence: a certainty that none of it ultimately matters:

> ...the world is not yet about to end but a
> recession is to come creeping in wearing
> faded tennis
> shoes

Everything pales into perspective when squared up against the great void of meaning that is the world, and the world itself is not about to end because something intangible can have no such boundaries to its existence. In effect, Bukowski manages in this poem to somehow break through to the other side of emptiness, to forge his way out the other side of the black hole and find there a serenity borne of the very same factors inciting panic back in the world of social oppression. An old man "lets out a little fart" and nobody cares, notices even, because it is all part of the moment, part of the whole that is the moment, and there is no disgust or etiquette or any other value judgements to disturb the simple peace of meaninglessness. It is almost as if Bukowski is himself as surprised as the reader at this discovery of peace beyond and yet inside the chaos of nothingness. He compares the cafe to "an accidental love", something floundered across by chance, but something with profound and lasting implications. It is a fleeting realisation of how life can be, but it is nevertheless a tangible one, and something the poet can carry with him as he "enter(s) the real world again".

In his essay on Bukowski, Armond Cheramie suggests that "chaos, madness and destruction is a vast process of letting-go which delivers us into the true realm of human existence". This is an opinion that indeed seems to be borne out by much of Bukowski's writing, although in the light of the poem just discussed, it is perhaps more fitting to say that it is emptiness rather than insanity that lies at the root of human existence. The quality of "beautiful wretchedness" that he remarks upon in the author's work, however, is certainly in evidence throughout, not least in the short story "The Life of a Bum". The hero, Harry, is presented to the reader as initially quite content, simply walking along the road at the beginning of the narrative thinking, "I am walking and I am smoking a cigarette". At its most basic level, Bukowski suggests, life is infinitely bearable. It is uncomplicated, free from stress and simply comfortable. Indeed, it is "the world [that is] unhappy", not the soul: the world of social form and regulation that has been created and built around the soul, confusing the simplicity of its being and bludgeoning it with class anxieties, greed, jealousy. There is a natural grace and instinctual logic about the way Harry attacks Monk and steals his money, pushing him in front a bus because he needs the cash, and the food it will buy, more than Monk does. It is a moment of impulsive action which exists outside the ethical order of society, and as such stands firm in its own animalistic survival instinct. Bukowski is careful to point out that Harry does experience some pangs from his conscience, that he does not act out of malicious or evil motives. By also stressing that "the guilt vanished", "like an old war finished", he manages to emphasise the amorality of this character, the way in which he is able to let the complex ethical influence drop and continue to exist outside of society's value system. This is certainly what is happening in this story, and is perhaps where Armond Cheramie comes in. Because good and evil are concepts just as morality and immorality are concepts. They are man-made, artificial notions that are superimposed onto a world that already exists in its own terms. The self-sustaining assumption bred by any society is that the laws and precepts it is founded on are intrinsically right and unquestionably just. It therefore follows that anything challenging these precepts is ultimately immoral, unjust, evil. Harry the bum is perhaps the one character in Bukowski's fiction who comes closer than any other to a state of real personal freedom simply because he exists beneath the moral codes of society, is depicted as an individual not in conflict with its values but simply beyond their grasp. He is neither good nor evil, virtuous or unjust, he simply is. "You [have] to find God first in order to find the Devil", "they [come] in that order".

So the closest an individual can come to liberty is through what is in effect chaos: by existing in a state of being somewhere below the ethical and intellectual processes established by society. Even this fails to some extent. Despite escaping the "terrified and disappointed", the "defensive and frantic" fate of so many others, Harry still has to pursue his life in a world where he is not accepted, where he can be told to "PAY UP AND GET THE HELL OUT" of a restaurant simply because he looks like he should not be able to afford the food he is buying, a fact that upsets the cook's understanding of the world. What is interesting, however, is that despite assertions such as these, ultimately defeatist in nature and seeming to suggest a nihilistic view of the world, Bukowski's ideological stance has still been variously interpreted as "religious", "leftist", and fundamentally moralistic. Whilst each of these can indeed be said to feature to some extent in the author's vision, none of them seem somehow adequate on their own, precisely because they are each too absolute, too rigidly structured into concise social perspectives and simplistic political theories. Neeli Cherkovski reports that Bukowski's main concern about the writing of the Beat Poets was "their engagement in social and political issues", that their poetry was somehow hampered by their fixation with "current affairs" and denied the depth that confrontation with "greater concerns" would have engendered. Indeed, Bukowski's own accounts of brushes with socio-political movements and ideologies are presented purely as reportage, fragments of a sort of social history of America which serve really to compliment the somewhat persistent theme of social mechanics that runs throughout his body of work. In *Notes of a Dirty Old Man*, for example, he focuses on the spate of political assassinations taking place in the sixties, conceding that "left wing liberal forces are being picked off one by one". The main thrust of his argument, however, is not overtly political in tone, but takes the form instead of a commentary upon the clever and manipulative manner in which those at the right wing of American politics react to these events. Governor Reagan, for example, takes the opportunity to blame any member of the populace who has any liberal tendencies whatsoever for allowing the laws of society to become too lax and enabling events such as these to happen. Of course, Bukowski is indignant, and rather than enter the messy world of politics for his answer, he instead cuts straight through the ideological swamp of Reagan's insinuations to the semantic heart of the matter:

> I neither killed Christ or Kennedy and neither did Gov. Reagan. that makes us even, not him one up.

It is indeed implied in the text here that Bukowski's political attitudes exist not on a proactive, issue driven ground-level, but rather in a more unspecific, high-level ideological status. In other words, whilst refusing to engage in specific political arguments, he leans towards a sort of vague socialism in his attitudes towards the equality of individuals ("what makes the governor himself so right and the rest of us so wrong?") and in his assertions that "men feel bad because life is bad for them the way it is" and "could easily be made better". This in fact seems a well balanced and infinitely reasonable perspective. When considering the concept of revolution, for example, his observations are of a distinctly rational and contemplative nature. "People get killed for nothing" he warns, and after much blood shed and destruction, "your new government is still the same old Papa":

> Before you kill something, make sure you have something better to replace it with.

What this discussion of revolutionary thought leads onto in fact in Bukowski's writing, is an examination of the American counter-culture during the sixties, to which the author applies the same critical eye and mechanical dissection that he uses elsewhere in his social critique. The story "The Birth, Life and Death of an Underground Newspaper", for example, chronicles the period of time that Bukowski spent, while still at the post office, writing a column for a counter-culture publication called *Open City*. His account is obviously a fictionalised one, but no less powerful a representation of the social climate of the sixties for this. From the first, Bukowski is keen to stress that although he is writing for an underground newspaper, he is most certainly not a leader, or even a member, of the hippie generation. "War is shit. War is hell" is an opinion he shares, and, he is careful to point out, an opinion he has had "for fifty years". The effect of this careful distancing technique is to basically liberate Bukowski from the single-minded, groovy values of his audience, delivering him back to the perspective he prefers: that of the objective outsider. And the effects of this can be immediately pinpointed in his writing, enabling him as it does to look both left and right; to assess simultaneously the cause, effects and influence of society on the counter-cultural socialist movement, and vice versa:

> ...this is America daddy, Hitler is dead. Or is he?

Bukowski's work is rife with representations of forces of social oppression, the Post Office, the father, the ethical zeitgeist, and so it is no great leap to compare the state and its many institutions of power to the fascism of Germany in the thirties and forties. The real trick here, however, is the way in which he then turns this inspection of values and systems onto the other side of the debate, onto the forces of social objection that he is supposedly supporting. He begins with a specific observation, noting that in the offices of *Open Pussy* (the apparent pseudonym for *Open City*) "everybody was starving for the Cause", or rather, everybody "except Hyans and his wife". Hyans is in fact the editor of the paper, and the fact that the head of the whole operation is working and suffering much less than his 'employees', begins to remind the author of the foremen and postal supervisors of the social system Hyans is supposed to be opposing. In the actual column he wrote for *Open City*, published collectively as *Notes of a Dirty Old Man*, Bukowski notes that in any revolution, there are "many in [the] ranks who would rather be president of General Motors than burn down the Shell Oil Station", and that "since they can't have one" of these options, "they take the other". This is precisely the same conclusion he comes to about the nature of the publication he in fact wrote this pearl of wisdom for. Hyans himself gives the game away at one point by referring to the supposed perspective of his paper as "all that pacifism shit". Bukowski seals the poignancy of this with the assertion that the structure of American society is just like "two bulls fighting for the cow": does not consist of an established social mechanism being challenged by a revolutionary faction who oppose its values and methods, but rather of a divided culture with both sides struggling for the same power and the same status in their own terms. In an interview with *Transit Magazine* in 1994, Bukowski indeed confirms that at some point the underground press "turned into a business"; that "they went

left-wing and liberal, because it was the young and proper thing to do", "they weren't really interested in it" for its own sake. He asserts here that "the real revolutionaries were never there" in the publications of the counter-culture, although this is a realisation he probably came to a long time prior to 1994, concluding "The Birth, Life and Death of an Underground Newspaper" as he does with the only regret upon its closure that "decency was in the streets again". "The cops had won, the city had won, government had won", and yet it is not the defeat of another potential order of society he bemoans, but the demise of an opportunity to offend. Just as elsewhere in his writing, Bukowski is not interested in taking on the might of an unconquerable social entity, but rather content to comment on its idiosyncrasies and limitations, exposing it for the fraud it is and warning his readership to beware.

In a letter which is freely bandied about the Bukowski community on the Internet, Kenneth Giles reveals what he considers to be the author's greatest weakness in the fact that "he mostly looked on life from a distance", that his perspectives existed for the most part outside of the social reality his characters inhabit and as a result he fails to engage with any one topic conclusively or convincingly. Linda King, the woman Bukowski fictionalises as Lydia Vance in the novel *Women*, indeed confirms on her website that "Bukowski [was] a person who changes", "a mass of sensitives (*sic.,*), egotism, uncertainties, confidence", a contradictory character who appreciated the fractured nature of existence and could not always perhaps reconcile the very different influences and textures of an infinite world. Rather than a weakness in his writing, however, this free floating vantage of the author's, noted by both Kenneth Giles and Linda King, is surely what empowers him to delve so deeply into the human psyche and the nature of reality. In the poem "Waiting", for example, he focuses upon the "hot summers in the mid-30s in Los Angeles", a time when he was "too young to be a man and too old to be a boy". He immediately places himself in a kind of personal limbo, partly associated with adolescence and partly because his world consists of "nothing to do" and "nowhere to go". Against his own inert state of being, Bukowski pitches the "socialists, communists, anarchists, standing on the park benches", ranting at each other and at the uninterested world. What makes this vision of Los Angeles so powerful is precisely the poet's detachment. There is emotion to be witnessed in the town, but it is all random and contradictory, and beneath it all there is just the "hot summers in the mid-30s in Los Angeles", the repetition of this description sounding over the poet's images of "starving dogs in the alleys" and worried parents like a tolling bell. The world contains this image and that image, the parks resound with this ideology or that ideology, but beneath it all it is just another hot summer in the same place with the same people and the same problems. In this poem, Bukowski uses his own state of being, unattached and unresponsive, to convey the state of the social world. America is caught in the grip of a depression; is caught in the languid stillness of a hot summer; is caught in a political inertia between a historical and an impending social upheaval, waiting with baited breath "as World War II move(s) toward [them]". The point is that the concept of politics makes an appearance in this poem, as does history, and morality as a neighbour tries to rob the Bukowski house and is caught by Henry Senior. All these notions weigh heavily upon Bukowski's Los Angeles of the mid-30's, and the poet recognises each of them, but is not swept ideologically along by any of them. They each have their place in the texture of reality, but they are all of equal importance and equal resonance and are all floating around a vast emptiness which is belief and purpose and existence and America.

> and everywhere is
> nowhere-
> the dream is as bad as
> flapjacks and flat tires:

Objectivity, then, is central to the poet's vision of the world precisely because he understands it to be a multifaceted reality with thousands of elements, none of them any more significant than any other, and precisely because it brings him closer to the meaninglessness which lies at the root of everything. In "The Blackbirds are Rough Today", Bukowski again pursues this method of representation: he deflates the reality of his world, asserting that "everywhere is nowhere", that there is no significance, no purpose, no connection to any part of the world's landscape. Indeed, it matters so little where anything happens (or doesn't happen) that the concept of place becomes redundant; the world becomes a dream of physical form in which nothing means, and by not meaning relates to every other thing that does not mean. In this manner he is able to correlate diverse strands of this reality and create of them a surrealist notion of his environment which perhaps comes closer to its true nature than any other mode of representation. Indeed, Richard Gray argues that "the extraordinary landscapes of post-war America can only be accommodated by a vision ready to use both fact and fantasy", which is certainly something Bukowski seems to agree with, comparing the ugliness of the urban reality with "flapjacks and flat tires", and the blackbirds to "ingrown toenails/

in an overnight/jail". There is a very interesting line in *The Buk Book*, written by Christy and Powell, where it is asserted that Bukowski ended his career (and his life) writing "about death and traffic", which rather than being a criticism, is in actual fact a remarkably accurate comment on the body of Bukowski's work as a poet. What Richard Gray overlooks in his poetry when he claims that "there are no large gestures" in evidence is the technique of inversion at work where Bukowski refuses to use the everyday occurrences of a character or a poetic self to connote the grand themes of the human condition but rather pulls the grand themes down to the level of the mundane:

> why do we go on
> with our minds and
> pockets full of
> dust
> like a bad boy just out of
> school-

It is almost as though the "bad boy just out of school" does not feature as an image to invoke musings upon the meaning of existence, but *vice versa*, the ultimate theological question narrowing infinitely down to a fine point of ordinariness and banality. Which is again linked into the understanding the poet has of his universe: the meaningless surface of reality is as significant and as insignificant as the ideologies and belief systems and divine purpose of life itself. Everything is relative and everything exists because of everything else and in order to facilitate everything else. Everything means and does not mean to precisely the same degree of importance, which is at once a liberating and a dangerously debilitating concept. Because "trying to code the madness into a simple number", trying "to understand life" is exactly what keeps so many people, including the poet himself according to his journals, in the act of living. To affirm that this is a pointless exercise is to destroy the only purpose there is. Except that perhaps the purpose cannot be destroyed. Perhaps to suggest that the chaos has no meaning is only to deflect contemplation from one pursuit to another: from that of finding significance to that of understanding insignificance. Bukowski warns that "we can't examine ourselves too closely or we'll stop living", and perhaps the new quest is then to know how much knowledge to seek and where to stop. The conclusion drawn in "The Blackbirds are Rough Today" is a typically inconclusive one, but then that is the nature of Bukowski's writing: explorative, deconstructive and questioning. The only thing certain is uncertainty, and the difficulty of defining something patently indefinable:

> I guess God meant it all
> like
> locks on
> doors.

Although this chaotic element of Bukowski's writing can be traced most easily throughout his poetry, it can also be found in his prose, particularly in his last novel *Pulp*. Here, he seems to move away from any semblance of realism, of plot or character development into a much more surreal and confused narrative which attempts to recreate the chaos of existence in more conceptual terms. Dedicated to bad writing, the novel takes the form of a detective story, a technique which at once realigns the focus of the discourse, setting it on a more inter-textual and symbolic plane than the author's previous work. The hero of the narrative is a Private Investi-

gator, conspicuously nonplussed by the events that occur around him, not unlike the stereotypical P.I. of film noir, and "the case is life", or so it would seem to be, because nothing that happens to him while attempting to work on his many cases seems to make any immediate sense. While searching for the red sparrow, a bird nobody has ever seen and the very existence of which is extremely doubtful, he finds himself hounded by both the female figure of Death and by a mysterious space alien who has powers of sexual attraction far stronger than any man can resist. There is also a confusion of cases in the narrative, with overlapping characters and plotlines that suddenly, for no apparent reason, simply resolve themselves. This, however, is precisely what Bukowski is trying to convey here, the fact that "existence [is] not only absurd, it [is] plain hard work", the effort lying in trying to figure out the chaos, trying to resolve the resilient and random events of a reality which adheres fastidiously to its own agenda. The detective in the story becomes a symbol of humanity, waiting and waiting and waiting for clues which will aid his understanding of the world; cutting a fine line between trying and resigning himself to fate. He knows that he cannot force meaning out a world that holds no such thing, and yet the effort involved in attempting to do this is perhaps the only thing that keeps a man sane, "chasing after a lot of nothing" precisely because "survival [is]…necessity".

In many ways, *Pulp* becomes for Bukowski an ideal vehicle to convey many of the issues his former novels touched upon in a much more blunt, concise manner. Whilst the convoluted plots serve to convey a perfect allegory of life, the fact that "none of it really [makes] sense", the manner in which issues resolve themselves, all inconclusively, also illustrates "the blank wall of the Universe". There are even attempts at a

clearly defined, deliberate humour which punctuates the ridiculous nature of existence:

> He had an ugly mustache (*sic.,*) and a false smile. Or maybe it was a false mustache (*sic.,*) and an ugly smile.

But what is perhaps most important about the novel is the way in which Bukowski defines the role of the writer in society. Because *Pulp* is very much a book about the act and the purpose of writing, creating as it does a purely textual world inhabited by icons and stereotypes of genre, and dealing as it does with issues of perception and ideology. The sexually attractive space alien, for example, seems to stand as a metaphor for another force of oppression and manipulation in society, that of overt sexuality or, in Bukowski's terms, women. Lady Death seems to denote void, chaos, nothingness. The hero finds himself at one point "sitting between Space and Death" "in the form of a Woman", the juxtaposition of concept and physical gender highly suggestive of the author's allegorical style here. What Bukowski seems to be doing is to create a specifically self-conscious representation of a broader reality, a world beyond the text that can only be understood, or not understood, in terms of the text. The universe itself simply exists; the world, America, Los Angeles simply exist as a series of colours, of textures, of ideas, of events. There is no intrinsic form to these features, no pattern or meaning, except that which the observer applies to them. In effect, every representation of the world is thus artificial, forged from the preconceptions of a defining mind. Which is precisely why a Private Investigator trying to crack the case of life is just as valid and just as poignant a retelling of the truth of existence as is any other

form of narrative. Of course, Bukowski then manages to undermine his own method in the very same stroke used to convey it. Not all of the metaphorical connotations engendered by the book, he warns, should be taken too seriously: "sometimes things are just what they seem to be and that's all there is to it". This, however, is precisely Bukowski's premise of the construction of the world: meaningful and meaningless at precisely the same time. He doesn't see any particular conflict in this because everything, including "insanity", "is comparative", everything exists in relative terms. And if the purpose of existence is to find a purpose, then there is no reason why discovering existence to be ultimately purposeless is any less a realisation of the original goal than any tangible aim would be. It is almost as though there is no such thing as a paradox in Bukowski's writing, only an ironic simplicity to life which manages to continually spark both a faint hope of contentment and a vague fear of defeatist inertia:

> you figure that everything is senseless, then it can't be quite senseless because you are aware that it's senseless and your awareness of senselessness almost gives it sense.

So Bukowski's writing seems almost to balance precariously on a fine edge of effort and stoicism: he sometimes urges action against the injustice of being, and sometimes suggests passivity, restraint from attempting to influence that which cannot be influenced. Quite often the world resolves itself regardless of precedent, and there is in any case no use wasting effort when things will ultimately be simply as they always are and simply as they always have been:

God over Man; Man over God. mother preserved strawberries while everything was so very sick.

In perhaps the most striking use of allegory prior to the writing of *Pulp*, Bukowski tells the story in *Notes of a Dirty Old Man* of an angel's short career with a local American baseball team, The Blues. Of course, this is no ordinary angel, and Bukowski immediately undermines its iconographic potential by referring to it as "the angel, or whatever", this uncertainty paving the way for reader interpretation which is precisely how the allegory in the story works anyway. What the angel perhaps symbolises above all else, however, is a chance for The Blues to stage a comeback, to turn around their losing streak and "get off the deck". He becomes a metaphor for an honest and tangible chance of success in a world in which success is rare, in a world in which society acts as an oppressive regime of status quo. "The strong make things go", the wealthy and the successful dictate the terms by which everyone else lives, and here is a very real opportunity to challenge and to change, if only for a short time, the unjust way things are. Except, of course, that the strong do not like to be disenfranchised, and react immediately when faced with a threat to their absolute domination. In the story, for example, the angel turns up drunk and in a distressed state for the final game of the season, the game that will decide the championship. "They sawed off my motherfucking wings". His drinks have been "loaded" in a nightclub; someone has "put [a] woman on" him, and then taken advantage of his distracted state to saw off his wings and cost The Blues both their best player and the all important game. What the narrative then becomes is both an illustration of and a diatribe against the social equation which dictates that wealth equals power and power equals success. Despite having a great baseball player, despite having an angel playing for them, The Blues are still subject to the whims of the unjustly powerful. The character Bugsy, the bookie who arranges the distraction and dismemberment of the angel, comes to symbolise the corrupt, wealthy business class which unofficially governs the terms of existence in the twentieth century American city. "A guy like me can piss in a mule's eye and come up with a mint julep". Wealth is the universal tool to get what you want out of life. With it, and the power it engenders, an individual is freed from consequence, is able to manipulate events to his favour and succeed however immoral the methods employed. Which is very much an integral part of the "all-American way of living and dying", but is not, Bukowski goes on to point out, the only power of influence there is. At the close of the narrative, with their star player incapacitated and any hopes of glory dashed, The Blues manage to win the game and the championship anyway. Bukowski, however, very interestingly refrains from drawing conclusions about the nature of irony, or luck, or fate, but instead turns his attention to something higher: "God beat man always...God being whatever It was". Instead of conceding that the structure of oppression that forms the spine of society is incomplete, that it is subject to unpredictable laws of chance that exist outside of its boundaries, he simply shifts the focus slightly, expanding the framework to include one more level. The working class is dominated by the state; the moral majority is oppressed by the corruptly powerful; the whole is subject to something else entirely - for want of a better term, God. Which is again a profoundly stoical perspective: if everything is ultimately subject to the precedents of something higher, then there is no point struggling against an order of reality that cannot be influenced. The manager of

The Blues, the narrator of the whole episode, tries to alter the order of being by blowing out the brains of Bugsy with a luger, and it is a futile action which merely results in his imprisonment. The Blues win anyway, and he is left sitting on a toilet in his cell in a world devoid of sense. The message here is very much the same message relayed through the narrative of *Pulp*: do not always seek to do, but instead sit back and let the world resolve its own issues in due course.

What this episode in the annuls of *Notes of a Dirty Old Man* also does, is to introduce the reader to Bukowski's ideological perspective of the female in American society. Here, a woman is used as an manipulative tool, a method of distraction whilst other business is attended to, and to some extent the author's use of women in his texts begins with this premise. Indeed, Russell Harrison suggests in his essay "Sex, Women and Irony" that Chinaski, Bukowski's hero in almost all his novels, constantly "feels compelled to make women into whores". Focusing upon a specific incident in *Factotum* where he attempts to pay a woman he has just had sex with, Harrison asserts that "commodifying the [sexual] act is the male's last-gasp attempt to maintain control", that women are for Chinaski/Bukowski nothing more than another face to the endless oppressive entity that is life. In *Women*, the author himself seems initially to support this theory, presenting the female as a cold force of being:

> Once a woman turns against you, forget it. They can love you, then something turns in them. They can watch you die in a gutter.

Except that this is something other than an illustration of oppression: it is rather an expression of the harsh facts of co-dependency and individual emotional detachment which constitute the ironic fabric of human relationships. Chinaski admits that he is "settled into nothingness", that life is essentially meaningless for him, and with this in mind thus craves "prostitutes, base women", women that are "deadly and hard and [make] no personal demands". If there is nothing worth caring about then there is certainly no point in subjecting oneself to the difficulties of love and relationships. Obviously, Chinaski experiences some sexual impulses and an occasional loneliness and craving for companionship, and throughout *Women* he seeks out various female characters to fulfil these needs and nothing more. Russell Harrison calls this "undeniable male chauvinism", but it is more of a sexual nihilism of Chinaski's than a conscious (or subconscious) prejudice on the part of the author. With no meaning to the world, there is no reason for Chinaski to think beyond the immediate moment of his existence. He lives almost on a series of whims, and his attitude to women is no more or less than consistent with this ideology:

> Once she had been a little girl, someday she would be dead, but now she was showing me her upper legs.

Existence is transitory and so emotions towards women are transitory and ultimately meaningless. Bukowski's attitude towards women is perhaps the most controversial aspect of his writing as a whole, even Linda King claims to have been repulsed by his sexism, his gender attitudes making her "furious, disgusted, indignant, sad". It is certainly an issue that resounds throughout any and all writing about the author and one which most critics cannot resist remarking upon. Russell Harrison is certainly no exception, claiming in one of his essays that Bukowski is in fact no more than "pseudo-macho": "the absence of positive women characters" in his work is no more remarkable than the absence of any characters, male or female, "with whom an intelligent reader...can identify". He goes on to theorise that Bukowski deliberately subverts popular precepts of the feminine by assigning his female characters knowledge that "would suggest more sexual experience than society feels comfortable with [them] having". Indeed, he seems to look upon Bukowski as an ironically feminist writer,

"questioning...rather than advocating, the attitudes and behaviour with which he has so long been (mistakenly) identified". Chinaski himself, however, admits of all his girlfriends and mistresses in *Women* that "each one of them was individual, different", and in light of this it is perhaps an exaggeration to attach a specific agenda to Bukowski's portrayal of the female. Ultimately, women are to Bukowski no more than another feature in a bleak landscape, another component to the complex world he inhabits. They are "human beings" like Chinaski, trapped in the same systems of injustice and conformity that he is, and if they represent somehow an other to Bukowski, it is not a totally alien other or a complete contradiction to his vision of the world. Women indeed fit rather neatly into the swirling complexity of issues that surround Chinaski. His take on morality, for instance, is simply expanded to accommodate the topic of relationships:

> People owed each other certain loyalties even if they weren't married. In a way, the trust should run deeper because it wasn't sanctified by law.

The same is true for meaninglessness:

> existence was a throbbing unbearable thing. I waited. I waited. I waited. I waited. I waited.

What is often seen by critics as a contentious issue in Bukowski's writing, then, is really no more than an unwillingness on the part of the author to elevate women above the level of meaning and meaninglessness that permeates the world of men. They too are part and parcel of the whole immoral maelstrom of values and selfishness and exploitation that simply is the social reality. Indeed, so resolute is Bukowski on this issue that perhaps the closest he comes to a love poem is the piece of verse in *Septuagenarian Stew* called "the summing up". Here, he begins by presenting his world as a rather empty and single focused one with an old hotel room as his environment and "the next bottle" his "apex", his "God". In many ways it is a typical Bukowski habitat, except that he then very specifically places his lover in the exact same locale: "the next bottle was all we scrounged for". It is not Bukowski who does the scrounging, but both Bukowski and his female companion. They are two of a kind; they "reinforce...each other":

she affected not to care about
anything and I went that way
too

If anything, he follows her example, not the other way round. The real point of interest, however, is that Bukowski doesn't degrade the female in his poem, instead he carefully constructs her as an absolute equal. To suggest that she is as worthy a human being as himself is perhaps the ultimate compliment that can be paid to another individual. Sure, she is far from perfect, "coughing around her cigarette" and

"singing", "cursing", "screaming". But in Bukowski's world perfection is never an option:

sitting in those tiny rooms
laughing, talking, choking, drinking, the
botch of us
like that-

Imperfection, the botch of life, is the medium we live in. "Near perfect" is as close as we will ever come to significance; discovering a momentary peace reading the Sunday papers as the world goes to work is as close as we will ever come to happiness, "Monday's millionaires" for an instant of time. In *Women*, he claims that "love is a form of prejudice", but here, love seems no more than a shared destiny. "We did what we did" is the conclusion to the poem, and conveyed in these five words is a sense of two people sharing the void of existence, drifting through a dream-like world together, bound with ties of languid affinity.

It is really no surprise to discover that the concept of human relationships in the work of Bukowski is at once a painfully simple and an infinitely complex one. This is after all the fundamental basis of his view of the universe: intricate systems of thought and oppression made all the more complex to disguise the vast void of meaning that lies within the foundation of the world:

> Now, it's a game of mirrors. And nobody is quite sure what is holding it together.

Relationships not only fit neatly into this model, but stand almost as a complement to it, are somehow further elements

of the same whole. Ironically, perhaps the best example of Bukowski examining the mechanics of relationships can be found not in his novels, or his poetry, but in his screenplay *Barfly*. Here, he documents an affair between Chinaski and Wanda, two social misfits who share "the understanding of the lost towards the lost". In much the same mode as the couple in "the summing up", they are seen to lead a half-life, a twilight existence somewhere between drinking and looking for the next drink. Chinaski's life is summed up at one point by Eddie, the bartender of the place he frequents, as "a bunch of can'ts (*sic.,*)", he "can't work,...can't fuck,...can't fight". Which is indeed partly true, except that Chinaski's and Wanda's refusal to subscribe to the standards of society is presented here as a rational decision, not a fundamental inability. Their lives are lives of "anti-meaning"; they have each discovered the absurdity of existence and are drifting along on its meaninglessness, unconcerned because concern is no longer an issue. Ironically, their nihilism makes for a remarkably liberated relationship: Chinaski is lead to the conclusion that individuality is paramount - "nobody owns anybody", and the couple develop a substantial level of trust very quickly, simply because "it's easier that way". There is a very real sense in the text (and on film) that the affection between the two characters is lent substance by the absence of obsessive emotions such as jealousy or vanity, an absence attributed by Chinaski himself to the fact that he (and Wanda) are "not pretending to be anything", are painfully honest about themselves and are not caught up in absurd social value systems.

And then there is the incident of the corn, which appears in the narrative of *Barfly* and is also commented on in the text of *Hollywood*. Jim Christy claims that Bukowski's "characters neither develop or stand in for Great Ideas", and whilst this may be generally true of his writing as a whole, it does not however follow that specific circumstances in the realist fiction never stand as allegories of existence in a wider frame of reference. In the case of Wanda, for example, the corn becomes a symbol of her entire life: it is sitting in the middle of an empty lot in the street, seemingly free and available, and yet is owned by somebody else, as "everything is owned". "There are locks on everything", everything is jealously guarded because material wealth is the American myth of success, and as Wanda steps up to take the corn she acts in a self-empowering manner, striking out against the rules of possession and dispossession:

> When she had screamed 'I want some corn!' it had been as if she wanted the whole world back, the world that she had somehow missed out on or the world that had somehow passed her by.

The world she has missed out on is one of success as defined through wealth and acquisition, and the blame for this can only be laid at the door of the social structure that has denied her any chance of achieving the very things it sets up as the pinnacle of human existence. She helps herself to the corn as recompense on a subconscious level for precisely this injustice, and is of course promptly pursued by the police for stealing. Wanda and Chinaski are then confined to their apartment, hiding whilst the police proceed to search the entire building for the thieves, and the incident becomes a metaphor for the lack of options available to those who exist at the baseline of a capitalist society. Commodities, here symbolised by the corn, are privately owned and are made available to others only at a price. To be unable to meet this price simply means that the commodity cannot be shared in, and to react against this wealth driven order of being and simply take what is required results in penalty by law. The poor individual in society is trapped by the paradox of commercialism which prices itself for the elite and then maintains the elite by excluding the masses:

> In a capitalistic society the losers slaved for the winners and you have to have more losers than winners.

This is why Wanda steals the corn and this is why both she and Chinaski are trapped inside their apartment, and yet she still comes away from the whole incident with a handful of corn which she then proceeds to cook. There is almost an air of success about the situation. Typically, however, Bukowski then punctuates the scene with a final token of futility and failure: the corn is unripe and inedible – the spoils of revolt are bitter and useless. Wanda's "life has been frustrating, and now the corn isn't even any good"; the trap is set too intricately to escape. The reason is perhaps twofold: primarily, the values of a society are so ingrained from birth that guilt follows closely on the heels of any transgression, however enthusiastically committed; secondly, an action borne of spite against the values of a society can only yield results that are ultimately of the same texture as the social order itself, results that exist in the same terms of reference as the very thing that was the original object of spite. So on a metaphorical level the corn is green and inedible because it is a part of the social order it was plucked from and it tastes as bitter to Wanda as is her perspective upon the order itself.

In *Hollywood*, there is a scene where Bukowski explains to

the actress who is playing Wanda on film that she was a woman who "never had a real chance" of success, and ultimately "didn't want one". On the face of it, this seems somewhat contradictory to her grappling for some recompense for her years of poverty and failure, but what the character of Wanda seems to move towards in the narrative of *Barfly* is precisely what Bukowski sets out it the poem "small cafe": an appreciation of the void that is existence. She is seen coming to terms with the powerlessness of the individual and how this can be used to forge the way through to the other side of being, creating a personal liberty out of the very thing that would seem to oppress it. The incident with the corn helps her to do precisely this, and it is also no accident that Bukowski casually drops into the text of *Hollywood* the fleeting remark about a life of "anti-meaning". This is really quite a significant term because it serves to instantly solidify a notion that runs right throughout the author's work and also sets the ongoing, sub-textual discussion on an almost scientific footing. Anti-meaning is like anti-matter, something that by definition doesn't exist, but by association must exist, polarity and opposition being a fundamental law of physics. With the assumption that meaning, significance, success and failure are all constructs of human understanding and human society, then anti-meaning becomes the alternative to this, the underbelly of the human psyche. Ironically, or perhaps not ironically at all, it is Lido Mamin, the dictator who features in a film Bukowski goes to see in *Hollywood*, who expresses this concept most succinctly:

> You think you know certain things but this is an illusion. You are only trained in one small area.

Of course, he's speaking of his own government from a

specifically fascist perspective, and yet at the same time he is speaking of the human condition itself. Because it is all one and the same: fascism is capitalism – "America, the beautiful" has its "human-skin lamps" too, only hidden in the dark rooms of the post office – and capitalism defines the system of values and social ethics that permeate the consciousness and govern the ideologies of a nation. So the things one knows are but the things one has been allowed to know; truth is no more than that which has been built into the tangible side of some equation of reality by the forces of oppression that exist only to perpetuate their own power. Anti-meaning is as close as Bukowski gets to revolutionary writing, as far along the route of expressing alternative modes of existence that he comes in his writing. Primarily, he is not enough of an idealist to imagine a system of social order that would work in a more beneficial manner to the working class. And secondly, he seems to regard such a task as too incomprehensibly large a job for any one intellect, proclaiming as he does to William Wantling in 1965, "the whole structure of everything is wrong so why pick at the parts?".

Raymond Carver has said of Bukowski that he was in life "a really strange guy", primarily because it was "almost impossible to agree with him". Even compliments made to the author about the quality of his work were met with sneers and insults – "I told him that I liked his poems", "he answered that I must have terrible taste". What this highlights, however, is not a distinctly eccentric man but rather the persona Bukowski has built of himself both within and outside of his text: the contrary old man; the gruff nihilist. Constantly seeking to offend because offence is comical and meaningless and words are the playthings of an insignificant people drifting through a vacuum of time. Beneath the surface of everything he finds a simplicity (usually an emptiness) which belies any superficial signs of complexity:

> I saw little meaning in anything and still have a problem with that.

Towards the end of his career he begins to examine this concept not only in social terms, but also in the realm of the self. Perhaps the most famous example of this can be found in the poem "the bluebird":

> there's a bluebird in my heart that
> wants to get out
> but I'm too tough for him,
> I say, stay in there, I'm not going
> to let anybody see
> you.

Here, it is not emptiness behind the façade, but something else which conflicts with the natural order of society: in this case idealism. This bluebird, this beautiful object, an icon of joy and hope and purity, is internalised by the poet and locked into his chest simply because he does not wish it to be publicly seen. He "pour(s) whisky on him", "inhale(s) cigarette smoke" and hides him from "the whores and the bartenders", both to protect the bird from a harsh reality which might destroy its frail form, and to keep intact the externally projected image he has constructed of a hardened man who cannot be hurt by the world. Whichever of these two motives is of the greater importance, the result remains the same: Bukowski has built a persona, has deliberately constructed an identity around what can be construed as a section of his true self in order to exist relatively undisturbed in the social world. He in fact makes of himself a nihilist out of necessity, forcing hope deep down into his subconscious where it can just about continue to exist:

> ...he's singing a little
> in there, I haven't quite let him
> die.

The trick to existing in a social world, according to Bukowski, is to do precisely this: to live in bare accordance with the terms dictated; to give nothing away but the minimum required; to know fully the rules of the world and to use them back against the world as often as possible. "The idea is to realize (*sic*,.) that a trap is a trap". "The trick is to work it enough in their directions to let you live, but enough in your direction to stay alive", "give an inch to take 400 miles". It is indeed a fine line to tread, but not an impossible one. "Death comes to those who wait and to those who don't", the only certainty in life being finality of its end and so to go on existing, in whichever way possible, is the only real option an individual has anyway:

> Death be damned. It's today and today and today.
> Yes.

So Bukowski's perspective on society is that it is a despicable creature, a complex system of lies and coercion that beats the individuality senseless and crushes the soul to conformity. And yet, it is all there is on offer, with the exception of death which is infinitely less preferable. As John Fante, perhaps Bukowski's greatest literary influence, puts it in his novel *Ask the Dust*, "it [is] better to be a live coward than a dead madman", and no matter how intolerable life seems to be, the only option left when everything is taken into careful consideration (revolution, non-conformity, death) is to "live...with the system", to give "a few honest hours" in return for the time and the money to drink and keep yourself sane.

The basic premise behind Bukowski's vision of contemporary American society is ultimately one of chaos, of emptiness, of meaninglessness. "We are eaten up by nothing" during every moment of existence, taunted by it and tormented by it. It reminds us that we "NOWHERE" and that "DEATH COMES WITH HIS LITTLE HANDS TO GRIP US" while we wait patiently, helplessly and insignificantly, for it to claim us. The purpose to it all is that there is no purpose, which is quite a liberating notion to the individual, but a horrific realisation for society as a collective consciousness, because the social world is founded upon the concept of effort, each member of the whole playing their part in a complex system of co-provision and co-dependency. If there are no longer any motives to do, then nothing will be done and the structure will fall. Which is perhaps not such a terrible thing, except for the great social institutions, and the people behind and inside of these institutions, who stand to lose the most from such a collapse of order and thus grapple for alternative methods of retaining power. These "Chosen in the land of the free" thus begin to perpetuate certain methods of ideological control in society, constructing ethical codes and value systems to breed in their populace a desire to conform and succeed, and conversely a fear of failure and a vague complex of guilt and shame. What this appreciation of the mechanics of society leads to for the author is a critical examination of precisely these values and morals which serve as stanchions for the status quo of power. Above all else, Bukowski seems to focus upon the fact of knowing as a means towards self-empowerment, as can indeed be seen in his remarks to his young daughter Marina:

> The policeman is very nice...but not all the time. There are also bad policemen, just like there are good criminals.

The emphasis here, as elsewhere, is not necessarily upon the lie of social precepts, but rather upon the false sense of singularity that often accompanies them. There is just as much chance that the policeman is not nice as there is that he is a great fellow; when contemplating the policeman, it does not automatically follow that the criminal is nasty. This is perhaps specifically an argument about semantics, but what it does illustrate is the tension in Bukowski's writing between alternate truths. The man's gravestone is apparently scribed with the words "Don't Try", but the author's vision sits precariously upon a fine edge of action and inertia; he deliberates endlessly between the "morals [that]...keep people slaves in factories", and the "morals [that] simply ma(k)e good sense". His position is not simply an objectionable one, but rather a probing one which seeks answers in a methodical manner from both sides of the equation. Bukowski is not a nihilist because he doesn't believe in anything, but because he believes primarily in Nothing, the eternal emptiness that we cram with meaning for our own sanity and for our own purposes, and from this vast cold space looks stoically out at the desperately forged intricacies of the human consciousness.

Neil Schiller
(neil.schiller@virgin.net)

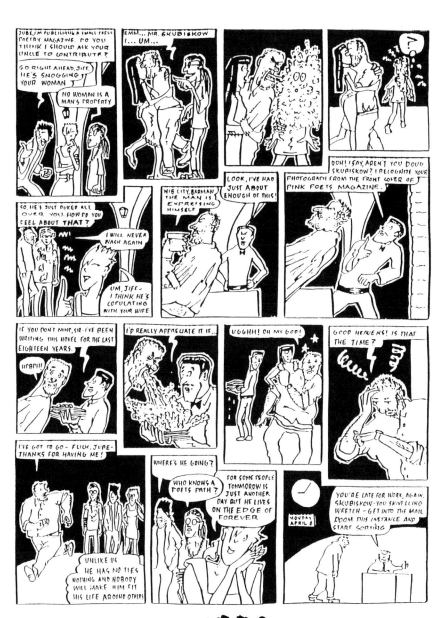

CULT BOOKS FROM MARION BOYARS

HUBERT SELBY JR.

'Selby's place is in the front rank of American novelists ... to understand his work is to understand the anguish of America.'
New York Times Book Review

Author of the controversial cult classic, *Last Exit to Brooklyn*, Hubert Selby is fundamentally concerned with morality. He offers a passionate empathy with the ordinary dreams and aspirations of his characters, a brilliant ear for the urban vernacular and for the voices of conscience and self-deceit that torment his characters.

SONG OF THE SILENT SNOW / ISBN: 07145 3050 6 / Paperback £9.95 / **THE ROOM** ISBN: 07145 3038 7 / Paperback £9.95 / **THE DEMON** / ISBN: 07145 2599 5 / Paperback £10.95 New Editions April 2000

GEORGES BATAILLE

'Bataille is one of the most important writers of the century. He broke with traditional narrative to tell us what has never been told before.'
Michel Foucault

Bataille's intense erotic prose fuses elements of sex and spirituality in a highly personal vision of the flesh. 'My Mother' illuminates a young man's incestuous passions, while 'Madame Edwarda' and 'The Dead Man' offer disturbing insights into human corruption.
Also by Georges Bataille and available from Marion Boyars are *L'Abbe C*, *Blue of Noon*, *Eroticism*, *Literature and Evil* and *Story of the Eye*.

MY MOTHER, MADAME EDWARDA AND THE DEAD MAN / ISBN: 07145 3004 2 Paperback £9.95 / New Edition April 2000

MARION BOYARS PUBLISHERS LTD
24 Lacy Road, London SW15 1NL tel: 0208 788 9522 fax: 0208 789 8122
email: marion.boyars@talk21.com www.marionboyars.co.uk

CHARLES BUKOWSKI VIDEOS

Bukowski On Film

by Steve Baker (sbaker1357@aol.com)

Seeing and hearing Bukowski live came late for me. At first I only saw other actors portraying him in various movie adaptions of his short stories before I stumbled across the man himself on video. I enjoyed seeing each actors take on Bukowski before I saw the real thing myself, it kind of added to the mystique.

CRAZY LOVE
(Mainline Pictures)

I was to find in my search there were various movie adaptions of Bukowski's stories around and top of the video pile for me is **Crazy Love** Although it doesn't include the old man himself, it's said to be Buk's favourite film adaption based on three of his short stories found in Ham on Rye & Tales of Ordinary Madness. In the film we see a man at three stages of his life. In the first, Harry Voss is twelve years old and naive, love for him is prince and princesses at the local cinema romantically in love and demurely kissing each other on the mouth...what awaits him in the real world is nothing like that! We see the gradual vision of the Bukowski males rites of passage beginning in 1955 with 12 year old Harry discovering the reality of female flesh then moving to 1962 when devastating acne removes him from any chance of female advances through to 1976 where our drink sodden hero is finally united with his blonde princess of his dreams -

a fresh corpse! You can see why it's Bukowski's favourite adaption of his work (hats off to it's Belgian film director Dominique Deruddere on his debut) because upon seeing the film, you immediately feel there's more going on than just Sex, Booze and Fighting which a lot of people rightly associate with a Bukowski film. For instance the acting is very tight, you really believe in the characters and the choices they make and it's moving to boot. In the middle film we see the main acne riddled character wrap himself in toilet roll at the high school prom and you can't help but feel for him even if the scene is quiet bizarre. The video cover uses this angle shouting "The most astonishing film debut since David Lynch's Eraserhead" It's a pity this still of the scene is used on the cover as it loses a lot of shock value when you actually see it, but non the less a great cinema moment. Be warned lowbrows, it is in sub-titles so have the remote handy when watching it on video, the action is so good you won't want to keep peering down to read it!

TALES OF ORDINARY MADNESS
(Art House)

Next up in the Bukowski film adaptions comes **Tales of ordinary Madness** This movie is in English and has Ben Gazzara taking the lead role of Charles Serking. I have to admit, I saw this film before I had heard any audio Bukowski so I always imagined this is what he would really speak like. (I read somewhere Bukowski thought Ben Gazzara went through the whole film looking like he was straining to have a shit!)
It's not a bad film as we see the down and out people and places of Los Angeles and self destructive relationships they ignite. Charles serking (Gazzara) is drinking himself to death

- he rejects all offers of help, preferring the freedom of the streets, the inspiration of the bottle and the excitement of brief, sexual encounters. When he meets the beautiful but mournful prostitute Cass (Ornella Muti) Serking begins to believe that love could redeem him by easing up the drinking and getting him writing again...if only. Cass has sunk even lower than serking and is trapped in a disturbing, downward spiral of self-hatred and mutilation which can only result in tragedy. The scene that really stays in the mind is Cass with her giant safety pin trying to adapt it into some sort of permanent chastity belt. Seeing a beautiful girl in such and ugly scene seems to add power to the moment.

Marco Ferreri's
Tales of
Ordinary Madness

The director Marco (La Grande Bouffe) Ferreri has come up with a graphic, disturbing, yet compulsive film. It runs at 100 minutes and although slow in a few places doesn't out stay it's welcome. My only reservation about the recent Video release was the piss poor cover. The first one I brought has a still from the film this time round we have a crap drawing close up of a pair of legs and a rose covering the beaver. It immediately gave it the film a mood of cheap tacky sex and the one still on the back of the blonde on the floor legs akimbo, although pleasing, did make it look like another one dimensional sex flick. Then again, maybe that was the idea to shift more copies this time round. Either way - check it out!

BARFLY
(Warner home video)

The film that probably brought more movie goers into the world of bukowski than the above two movies put together was **Barfly**. Directed by Buk's friend Barbet Schroeder and staring (at that time) regular Hollywood stars Mickey Rouke and Faye Dunaway. Bukowski wrote the screen based on an earlier period of his life when Jane was the main player in the relationship in buks life. We see Henry Chinaski (Rouke) cruising the seedy night-time streets and bars of L.A., boozing and brawling sharing his disgust with humanity with who ever's prepared to listen. Ultimately ending up back in his room. Then we find him emptying his pockets of scribbled poetry. This is the gradual emergence of bukowski the writer born on scraps of paper, poems inspired by the madness of his life hanging around bars and getting into fist fights. The scenes work well in the dingy boarding rooms, especially when Chinaski goes for a piss then returns to the wrong room. He doesn't realise until he opens the fridge and finds it's packed with food and booze. Improvising he takes as much as he can wrestle with back to his own room. Each time I see this Mickey Rouke portrayal of Henry Chinaski I think something different. When I first saw him I thought it was well over the top portraying Hank as a bedraggled tramp which we all know he wasn't. Then the next time I saw in his performance a sort of WC Fields cartoon, the Neanderthal poet who's eventually wined and dined by the establishment of society magazines which he rejects seeing it as just another bird cage to entrap him, albeit with Gold bars instead of damp rusty ones.
you might be well advised to read the Black sparrow Book of the screen play (reviewed else- where in this publication) before seeing the film and it does in fact read well on it's own. Give this film a go, it just been released in the Maverick directors series - which Barbet certainly was. He threatened to cut of his fingers with a chainsaw if the backers didn't put up the full amount of money needed to make the movie. Just like a character might in a Bukowski poem.

CHROME DREAMS

www.CHROMEDREAMS.co.uk
PO Box 230, New Malden, Surrey, KT3 6YY
Fax: 0208 241 1426 **e-mail:** mail@chromedreams.co.uk

**"NEWSPAPER TAXIS: A Bizarre Ride to the Dark Side...
Drugs, Cult Authors and the Boho Zone."**

As a passenger aboard this magical mystery trip, you will hear the voices of:
Timothy Leary, Aldous Huxley, J.G. Ballard, Kenneth Anger, Brian Aldiss, Ken Kesey, Martin A. Lee, Philip K. Dick, Gordon Liddy, William Gibson, Bruce Stirling, Lawrence Sutin, William Burroughs, Allen Ginsberg, Tom Disch and H.R. Giger

Catalogue Number: EN 9001   ISBN 1-84240-001-0

"TALKING HEADS
Great Speeches from the First Century of Recorded Sound"

A fresh, modern look at some of the great speeches of the Twentieth Century including Winston Churchill, Adolf Hitler, John F. Kennedy, Princess Elizabeth, Richard Nixon, Neil Armstrong, Gloria Steinem, Neville Chamberlain Franklin D. Roosvelt, Malcolm X, Harry Turnan, Edward VIII, Adlai Stevenson and Martin Luther King.
Catalogue Number: EN9002 ISBN: 1-84240-003-7

"DIGGIN' THE NEW BREED
Accounts of the Inspirational Power of Madness Versus the Clean Life:
The Beats and Postwar America."

In 1943 three men together formed the most potent underground art phenomenon of postwar America. Jack Kerouac, William Burroughs and Allen Ginsberg would create a movement which explored the capacity for joy and liberation which lay in the collective psyche. Their method: music, literature, sex, drugs and crime. Their goal: personal freedom. Their password: rebellion.
Catalogue Number EN9004 ISBN 1-84240-004-5

Titles are priced at £6.99 inc VAT, postage and Packing inside the UK (add £1.00 for overseas) Please make checks payable to Chrome Dreams at the above address, fax credit card details, or alternatively visit our website at **www.chromedreams.co.uk** to order direct.

THE BUKOWSKI TAPES
(Lagoon)

This video is a four hour opus of Bukowski filmed mainly in his house and garden in San Pedro drinking beer and smoking small cigars as he chews the fat with Barfly director Barbet Schroeder in the cool evening air. We get along the way also to see the house where buk lived with his parents, Hollywood Blvd and various old haunts frequented by the dirty old man. As you watch (over a cool beer) you get the feeling Bukowski is very relaxed with barbet as he talks about different moments of his life from being alone, the police, booze, women, shitty rooms, shitty jobs and so on, even finding time to read a few poems including one of my favourites of existential angst: the man at the piano.
As the conversation flows you begin to get the impression in the bukowski drawl an underlying weariness, the voice of a man propping up the bar around 2 am, a man who's been there and done it yet still has the fire of a belly laugh at the absurdity of it all or where he sums up something in the most erudite way then shoots himself down...as he knows, it's all words yet...there's something just beyond. Probably harder to reach talking to someone than putting down in a poem, but Buk comes damn close a couple of times. You'll all have your own favourite moments, some people say things better than others to different ears.
In total there's 52 segments of Bukowski, shifting from the reckless to the sublime all in the drag of a cigar and gulp of a beer. It keeps your attention that is apart from the annoying piano break between the segments (same piece x 52 = Arrgh!) It's a real Bukowski treasure trove, an important document of Bukowski that really gets behind the man and his views in a natural way. So all in all we should be grateful

The CHARLES BUKOWSKI Tapes

PRODUCED AND DIRECTED BY
BARBET SCHROEDER

GRAND PRIX
SALSO
MAGGIORE
TV/VIDEO
FESTIVAL

to Barbet for having the inclination to film it in the first place and let buk's answers just flow spontaneously rather than using the clipped chat show format most might have expected. As Barbet himself says:
'I spent three years in Los Angeles, working on a film project based on an original screenplay of Bukowski's Barfly. I couldn't stand the thought of not being able to share the extraordinary evenings we spent together. I finally brought in a small crew, friends of mine, with some high quality video set up for some of our sessions...whoever was the least drunk took care of the camera. Over the years, I collected fifteen hours of tape this way. Almost all of it was useable. Charles bukowski had true natural presence that the great actors might envy. I wanted to keep a tight shot on his face and the music of his words. To try to show that behind his reputation as a degenerate and old drunkard, which he helped to establish, was a poet of exquisite sensitivity, who was hard on himself. A poet of shattering lucidity and also of great wisdom. However, these aims were incompatible with the standard format for TV shows. The material itself held the solution to the problem. I realized that as I don't like formal interviews, I had constantly tried to just get him started on a topic and then keep from interrupting him. The result was often a monologue of three minutes or longer. The ideal way to show this material then, was in short video clips - a new style of film. Once I had screened it this way, it seemed twice as powerful. Naturally, Bukowski is violently opposed to what is said and thought in America today, even in anti-establishment circles. A few months ago, during a long evening together, we watched all 50 clips. He remembers nothing of what he said on the tape. He was truly astounded. A couple of times, I felt him flinch and hold his breath. On screen he seemed to be talking seriously about

important things but the humorous note that redeems everything always came and Hank heaved a sigh of relief. As did we, buk still had the magic.

BUKOWSKI AT BELLEVUE 1970
(Visionary)

So having seen bukowski for the first time in the barbet Schroder's Bukowski tapes, it was interesting to then see him way back in 1970 at Bellevue college USA when this film was recorded. Upon watching it you do get the impression of slight nervousness in Bukowski but this is only his fourth reading remember as he tells the audience "Im pretty raw". This nervousness might also be due to the fact that he doesn't have anything between himself and the audience except his books of poems and a flask of coffee. In later readings when he'd at least have a desk to lean on you could feel he was more at home, less 'naked'. That said we still get the laid back bukowski drawl are some excellent moments not least toward the end when he reads Fire Station (for Jane with love) Bukowski really seems to enjoy telling this one and uses the different male / female voices to effect. Even the nervous audience laugh in the right places. Due to the age of the film there are moments it freeze-frames in one spot and the voice continues, but this plus the raw black and white footage certainly adds to the mood.
All in all a good document of man and crowd, who it must be said, seem pretty respectful of old hank compared to later readings where heckles and shouting of abuse would come thick and fast. Mostly from Bukowski himself!
The browny yellow tinted video sleeve is pretty darn good showing a photo of Bukowski in a downtown Los Angeles street circa 1970 leaning against a religious paper stand

while on the back we see Buk in 1965 leaning in the door frame of his room in new Orleans with his two best friends to hand. Beer and smokes. I guess we should leave the final summing up to Black sparrow publisher John Martin :
In the spring of 1970 Charles Bukowski, then little known, packed his overnight bag, locked the door of his tumbledown East Hollywood apartment behind him, and took his first plane ride to the state of Washington to read at Bellevue College. This pioneer reading (only his fourth ever) was videotaped in black & white using two camera's by students and the film lay forgotten for 18 years.
While the technical aspects of this film are shaky, all of this one hour reading comes through loud and clear. Here is Bukowski, at mid-life but at the beginning of a great career, reading powerfully and with grit and humour. A once in a life time moment has been rediscovered and preserved forever.

THE ORDINARY MADNESS OF CHARLES BUKOWSKI
(Bookmark)

This documentary was originally show on the BBC's Bookmark series and is an ideal way for people new to Bukowski to understand the man and the myth. It contains various clips from Barbet Schroeder's Bukowski tapes and original material such as interviews with people from different stages of Bukowski's life. These include his publisher John Martin who came across as very down to earth, easy going, then his wife Linda Bukowski who was very spiritual (Im sure she could see the Zen-ness in a lot of Bukowski's writing) to his daughter Marina who I felt came across with a really good 'take it or leave it' attitude towards her famous dad's writing. Of course a lot of the film world loved Bukowski and at

the start we see Sean Penn reminiscing about a party he went to with Buk. The fact that the house it was held in is no longer there couldn't have been down to Bukowski getting out of hand surely!?? Sean Penn is clearly a big Bukowski fan (he also likes Ed Bunker, Harry crews & Krishnamurti - good taste) although Im not sure about the part where he analyses Buk drinking from a bottle (Buk puts a bigger tilt on it than most when pouring it down his neck...sign of a real drinker?) But best of all is when we get to see two co-workers from Bukowski's past from the post office. Fact and fiction merging. The old lady say's Bukowski gave her a poem on a piece of paper one day at work but she lost it...this part I found really interesting because here we see someone from his old days actually seeing him now and how he progressed from then. I wish I had of kept it she said. So do we!

We get to see Bukowski at home squeezing oranges from his trees and yelling Linda to 'come and get your juice!' and this maturer Bukowski is balanced through out by some great footage of various barflies and lost souls in various bars and pool halls looking like they just stepped out of a Edward Hopper painting. Strangers in the Night was never put to a better film clip, it still makes the hairs on the back of my neck stand up....what a dancer! Can he write as well as he moves?

DOCUMENTARY BY TAYLOR HACKFORD

I haven't been able to find a copy of this film yet, if anybody can point me in the right direction I'd be most grateful. I understand it contains about 30 minutes of black and white footage where we see Bukowski doing a poetry reading, buying beer and being interviewed. That's as much as I can tell you folks.

ANY OTHER BUKOWSKI ON FILM...?

Well that's what I'd like to know? Can any readers out there help make this Bukowski film review complete? I did hear somewhere Bukowski did a narration on a film about Skid row?
Anyone who can help with this, the Taylor Hackford and any others - please get in touch via e-mail or write c/o Buk Journal. Thanks!

Sbaker1357@aol.com

Henry Charles Bukowski
by Michael d. Meloan

When I was fifteen years old, my friends and I cruised Sunset Strip and brought back the underground papers with Notes of a Dirty Old Man. We sat inside a plywood shack that one of the fathers in the neighborhood had built in the back yard to keep us out of trouble. We'd smoke, and drink, and read Bukowski's column out loud. It was an explosive fire hydrant spewing philosophers, hookers, madmen and race track junkies.

Sixteen years later, my girlfriend was working in a small health food restaurant in south Redondo Beach. She mentioned that the owner, Linda Beighle, had recently started dating a poet named Charles Bukowski. I went to the Dew Drop Inn for an alfalfa sprout sandwich, and left with an invitation to Bukowski's annual 4th of July barbecue.

In the fall of 1982, he invited me over for the evening. Just the two of us, and his plastic goose with a light bulb inside. Linda was living with him, but had gone to the east to visit her family. He uncorked the first bottle of wine.
"You seem a little nervous," he said, pouring.
I took a BIG drink. I was nervous. But in a few minutes, the night took off like a rocket. We were laughing and drinking until three in the morning. He lit his eye brow instead of a cigarette, and growled like an animal. He told me later that I danced with the goose on my head, and recited a long raving monologue. I don't remember, but he

always did.

If you knew Bukowski, you called him Hank. He was Henry Charles Bukowski Jr., but he detested the sound of Henry. It echoed with the memory of his father screaming that name during their many confrontations. But he did use Henry as his first person alter ego Henry Chinaski, which appeared regularly in his reality based tales of extraordinary people trapped in dismal circumstances.

Charles Bukowski was the writer. The middle name Charles gave him some distance from the process of creating his world in print. He published nearly fifty volumes of poetry and prose during his 73 years.

The wild Bukowski was not completely overstated. At one of his 4th of July barbecues, he got an early start drinking, and decided that the party was a bore. He walked around the living room, demanding, "Where's your drink!" A balding man in a cardigan sweater said, "I don't drink." "Then get out!" said Hank. "In fact, I want everybody out! I'd rather be upstairs typing." The group thought it was a joke at first. Then he ran around the rooms screaming, "Get out! Get out!" until the house was empty.

As people slowly walked down the long driveway, two tall young men approached me, and asked in heavy German accents, "What is happening? What is happening?" They were part of a frequent pilgrimage that German tourists made to the house. "He threw everybody out," I said laughing, "because we weren't drinking enough." "This is very cool," said the German. "Very Bukowski!"

In a one-on-one encounter, Hank demanded your full attention, even when he was drunk. Sitting on the couch in the living room, he would take a drink, then a drag, and his eye would cut over at you. Scrutinize you. There was no place to hide.

He was a complicated man. Outrageous and sensitive. Loyal to his friends in the most important ways. If you called him for advice, he would give you everything he had.

Two years ago, Hank wrote me a letter about literary agents, and writing in general. He finished it with..."The whole thing comes down to this: if you want to write, you're going to write, and you're going to write it your way. If you're after money or fame or groupies or ???..then that's something else, then you're going to do it their way, and they will smash you down into a flattened turd." At the bottom, he signed, "The old man has spoken. Ring the bells of the city. uh-huh." And he had drawn himself walking, with a big sun up above, and two dogs at his feet. A bird was flying at the top of the page.

On Monday March 14, 1994, I attended Hank's memorial service on a rolling green hillside overlooking the San Pedro Harbor. Buddhist monks chanted while his wife Linda stood next to the casket. Hank was buried in the clothes that he always wore to the race track. A felt tipped pen in his shirt pocket to mark the racing forms.

- Michael D. Meloan (Email: Mdmeloan)

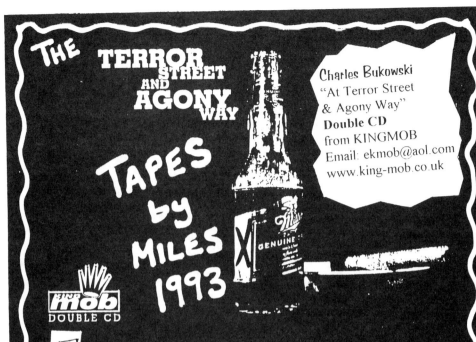

The TERROR STREET AND AGONY WAY

TAPES by MILES 1993

DOUBLE CD

Charles Bukowski
"At Terror Street & Agony Way"
Double CD
from KINGMOB
Email: ekmob@aol.com
www.king-mob.co.uk

These tapes are the result of an abandoned, but not forgotten, recording project I began in 1968 about which the less said the better. I had been an admirer of Buk's work since 1965 and finally had a chance to record him. So it was in February 1969 I pulled up at 5125 1/2 De Longpre Avenue in a slummy part of East Hollywood near the 20th Century Fox Studios on Sunset in a rented green Mustang which looked gleamingly conspicuous in the shabby street. Slums in Los Angeles are not like those of other cities. During the Watts riots a few years before, the foreign press had driven straight through Watts looking for the slum because to European eyes these are reasonable houses: everyone seems to have a large car and a television, it's always sunny and there are palm trees lining the streets. It is not the South Bronx, it is only a slum in contrast.

De Longpre was made from large slabs of concrete, chipped at the edges, lined with utility cables and tall scruffy palms, some of which had died and rotted. The single storey wooden frame houses had peeling paint and there were holes in the screen doors. Bits of cars lay in front yards and rubbish blew about. A '57 Plymouth was parked on the ruins of Buk's front lawn. Beercans overflowed his garbage bins.

The screen door opened straight into his living room. The shades were drawn. Rickety bookshelves were overloaded with books, magazines, old newspapers and racing forms. The settee had a hole where the stuffing was bursting out. There was a pile of car tires in the corner and many empty beer cans, and in another corner was Buk's desk. Here was Buk's typewriter: a prewar, battered, sit-up-and-beg, black cast-iron Remington; dusty but for the carriage and keys which were polished by use, surrounded by cigar butts and ash, crumpled paper, extinct beercans. Hundreds, perhaps thousands of poems had emerged from that old machine; countless stories, columns for Open City, the local underground newspaper which had been running his "Notes Of A Dirty Old Man" column since May 1967, and letters to every little mimeographed poetry magazine editor who contacted him, from Germany to Japan, mid-west farm-boys to slick New Yorkers – hundreds and hundreds of them.

Bukowski seemed happy to see us, (I had my assistant Pat Slattery with me), but immediately after finding seats for us he was off, slipping like a shadow through the door, across the porch and away. Soon to return with another 6-pack. Now he had a smile on his face and a bottle of Miller Light in his hand. He found a glass for Pat in the messy kitchen in back, talked about the race-track and about his publisher John Martin, from the Black Sparrow Press, about little poetry magazines and his worries and fears about trying to make it as a professional poet. Essex House, the pornographic book publishers, had just released a collection of his pieces from Open City, called Notes Of A Dirty Old Man as a mass market paperback, (or as mass market as a company that published books with titles like Thongs was likely to get) and he was encouraged by this latest development.

We talked about the record. He was casual, relaxed and said that he had made a lot of home recordings before: "Sure, just show me how the machine works and come back in a few days. I'll just curl up on the rug with some packs of beer, my books, turn on the machine and... " I wired up an Ampex 3000, arranged a microphone stand and microphone, headphones and 12 reels of blank tape. He refused to allow me, or anyone else, to be present to supervise the recording, claiming to be too shy. Some of the problems he had with the equipment are spelled out in his between track comments on these CDs, most of them caused by his attempt to record on "both sides" of the tape which wiped what he had previously recorded.

Nine days later my assistant from San Francisco, Valerie Estes, and I pulled up in a blue rented Mustang. Buk was there, a bit hung-over, and so was a woman, middleaged, wearing black fishnet stockings and a black slip. She disappeared into the bedroom without speaking, emerging some time later ready to leave, looking tired and worn. Buk crushed some notes into her hand. "Carfare" he said, as much to me as to her. Nothing in the room had changed. The Ampex was where I had left it but it was done; every reel was filled with Buk's careful selection from his writing – six hours of his favourite pieces. He said to be sure to listen to the one called "The Firestation" as he liked that best of all. Then he told us a long story about his '57 Plymouth

and about his landlord, flirted with Valerie, and eventually we got everything packed up and he helped carry it out to the car. A few days later, at the end of February 1969, Pat Slattery came by with a photographer and took the photographs you see here.

I agree with Buk that "Firestation" is the best track, because it has that mixture of tenderness and toughness, understanding and acceptance which characterise his Buk's best work. I really like these tapes because they were recorded before he became a "professional" writer. He had made a few tapes before, but these still have the conversational quality of someone who had not yet read his work in public. There is no attempt at performance other than getting the poem across. It happened that this was a turning point in his career. A few weeks after making this recording he gave his first poetry reading. A year later, on January 2, 1970, at the age of 49, he finally quit his job at the post office and devoted himself full time to writing. He couldn't get away from the post office, however; it became the subject of his first novel, called, unsurprisingly, Post Office published by Black Sparrow in February 1971.

Most people discovered Buk through the novels: Post Office, Factotum (1975) and Women (1978) with their gritty, erotic, uncompromising and above all, honest, portrayal of life at the bottom. They are in the tradition of Jack Black's You Can't Win or John Fante's three volume saga of Arturo Bandini (a major influence on Buk). His work stands alongside William Burroughs' Junky, Herbert Huncke's Guilty of Everything, the humour of Lenny Bruce, the growled vocals of Tom Waits, solos by Chet Baker or Art Pepper, the Beats and the deadbeats, the drop-outs and the freaks: white American males living in the underside of society, telling their experience with compassion and humour.

Bukowski started afresh, made a new life, got a new wife, began to drink fine wines instead of six-packs. He left deLongpre. He gave readings on smart college campuses and his books appeared in signed limited editions with paintings by him on the half-title. In 1987 Hollywood released the movie Bar Fly with a screenplay by Buk. His experiences working in tinseltown, which he didn't particularly enjoy, were recorded in Hollywood. He is still writing. He is doing all right.

Miles, London, 1993

Drinking The Buk
by John J Martinez

I stretch out my arms, and breathe in the air. I realize for the first time today that I'm alive, and I'm ready. They call my name and I rush on stage, and as the applause dies down, I look around. The audience, those kids, those elders in the corner, They're all waiting for me to saying something, and by God I'm gonna give 'em what for tonight...

When I write, I think about him. It's not on purpose, but you can't help but feel that he's out there, somewhere, waiting for you to run into him, and to say that you want to buy him a drink. I'm not sure he'd smile, but I think he'd accept the gesture, and then drink the thing in front of you, and not say thank you or anything. That's him. That's the guy. He wrote it. He lived it. He's Buk.

I expected to run into him when I went to Seattle, Washington last year. I had some time off, so off I went on a Greyhound bus out west to soul search. 3000 miles and two days later, I was back in the city that first woke me to the arts, the scene, the life I should have been living from birth. I was in the army then, over fifteen years ago. God, fifteen years, and here I was.

I checked into a hotel that didn't ask any questions (the Commodore Hotel, I highly recommend it) and I was set to conquer the town. But what was I looking for? I was a bit of a minor celebrity in my hometown, and was given the courtesy of reading my poetry before others not so well known, but what was the missing piece? That's when my best friend Lance introduced me to him. Read him, he said. I read

"Mockingbird Wish Me Luck," I read "Love Is A Dog In Hell." I was exhilarated! Who was this guy? I went to libraries, and bookstores, and found his books are the most stolen worldwide. One of his books alone have reprinted more times than all of the re-printings of "On The Road" by Kerouac, or "Howl," by Ginsberg. He is beloved in Germany,
and Europe can't get enough of him. Why? Why haven't I ever heard of the bastard? The problem then presented itself to me. I MUST find all of his writings. He was surly, he wrote when he drank, he hated celebrity, but when he drank he had to be the center of the universe, or there would be arguments, and fights, and arrests. He hated other poets and their pretentiousness. He disliked men who came to him, kissing his feet, playing up to his sentiments. He often threw them out. And here I was in Seattle, writing poetry, visiting my son (from a previous mistake), and wishing to God that I could be half the writer he was. Maybe I was, though, and just didn't know it. I went to open mike poetry readings while I was there, and I sold copies of my two books of
poetry, but when I was done, I still drank alone. I drank beer, got wasted, then slept it off. I did this for a week. I dreamed about my past, almost similar to his. My old man never told me he loved me, I think. He was drunk a lot of times whenever he would come home from selling life insurance from his sorry office, sleeping with whores on his lunch breaks, and treating my four brothers and I like a cleaning crew to show off at parties. My mother tolerated this shit for years, now a destroyed woman. He would abuse us, then sleep it off. He was always so repentant in the morning, almost kind. When he finally ran off on us, he was still repentant to the end. I began writing poetry since then, poems about being that close, so close to the love, and the truth, but

not reaching it. About loss and anger and repression, and tears and sweat and fear.
Everybody's childhood was like this, right?
Years later, when I would read his book, "Ham on Rye," it came crashing home. With every page, I returned to my childhood, and regretted the words, the arguments, the broken furniture, and his final escape. I was alone, and sure, women and children are abused every day, but I never told anyone about it. His book explained pain in a way I couldn't, especially the beatings. Then suddenly, sitting in a hotel room in Seattle, I became possessed, and I began to write it out, the atom bombs in my heart exploding into a bloody mess all over the pages, and I was propped up by him, Buk and his books pushing me forward to face it, his words drumming into my ears through video and tape and albums, the images of drunkenness I remember after my divorce all over the movie "Barfly". And I remember sitting alone, writing while drunk, drinking in bars all up and down Yakima, Washington (find that one on a map), feeling crazy, sitting in my kitchenette apartment, the music blaring, the noise keeping me from losing it, and realizing I was finished, and writing about the loss in my poetry. All of these ugly drunken images came forth like a good vomit onto the page, needing to. For seven days in Seattle, I also got over it and read, read, read. I also wrote about the present, the loss, the anger, and it sounded real for once. My obviousness in my first two books dissipated. I then read about his "Women," I learned to "Run With the Hunted," and I found out that having a job isn't too bad of a fucking thing in "Post Office," but it isn't everything, either.

I went home, a backpack full of books, and pages, and broken ink pens, and my sanity, although I had to see if I could pull it off. I arrived home and devoted myself to drink-

ing up every word he had to say, and not because I was some college asshole needing a hobby to explain his dullness in between sleeping around and waiting for daddy's check to clear. Buk woke me up to myself.
I was a guy who worked in hops factories and slaughter-houses, Hell, I never even finished two semesters in college. Buk was the propellant to get me going. I found my fire from inside and I have to thank him. I drink now to know better. I get out of my head to find it. I don't read books all the time anymore, because he said not to. I'm open, and I drink it all in.

...So here I am on stage, ready to go. I hold up my newest poetry book, my "Ham on Rye," and I go into it. They're amazed, I think, because I was always the clown, the joker, laughing like an idiot. Now I'm not. I finish and they applause, wondering what happened. I realize the joke always has been on me, but I don't have to laugh all the time. I drank
 Buk, and now I'm drunk- on my life.

       John J Martinez   (e-mail: Poetryy2kman)

BUKOWSKI & CENSORSHIP (X)
By Wilfred D. Day

Bukowski gained a following with his crazy stories and (Probably) real life antics in the late 60's columns: 'Notes of a Dirty Old man' written in the columns of *Open City* a Los Angeles free press newspaper. So much so that eventually his boss at the Post office where he worked, called him in for a little chat. I guess the heading of the columns, Notes of a Dirty Old Man was a bit of a give-away. But our hero need not have worried, readership and word of mouth notoriety were growing to such an extent that eventually by 1969 the collection of columns were collected and published in book form by City Lights Books of San Francisco under the same title Notes of a Dirty Old man. If you had never heard of Bukowski, the title was sure to let you know what you were in for if you chanced upon the book!

As Bukowski said in the intro: "I am just an old guy with some dirty stories. Writing for a newspaper, which like me, might die tomorrow morning. It's all very strange. Just think, if they hadn't airbrushed the cock and balls off the Christ child, you wouldn't be reading this!"

This encapsulates for me what is so good about Bukowski's writing, in this above statement he puts across the censorship debate succinctly: ie. If people didn't get so up-tight about nudity - you wouldn't have so many writers / artists going the other way and exploiting our *learnt* reaction to it. Yin and yang, Black and White, God and Devil, Sex pistols and Mary Whitehouse etc. It's the contrast which defines them. The stronger the opposite - the clearer the definition. So am I a repressed person who need's to counter this repression with Bukowski? Nah, there's a lot heavier shit out there than Bukowski's, but sadly is just drivel to read.

Of course not all the writing of Bukowski has a message, I guess you get out of it what you put in. This was another redeeming thing about Buk, (and Kafka, Beckett, Philip K Dick who I also really rate) the sense of humour lifted him out of the Hemingway / Henry Miller/ Kerouac dry school of writing. Bukowski was direct and un-cluttered which left room for different moods to interpret his words. Hemingway, Miller and kerouac on the other hand seemed like one trick ponies to this reader. Once you'd read one of their books, you'd read them all.

But as we said earlier about opposites, I guess they make Bukowski look even better!

Wilfred D. Day

A ROUGH GUIDE TO THE "BOOKS OF A DIRTY OLD MAN"

CHARLES BUKOWSKI READS HIS POETRY AND 2 1/2 SLICES OF MUSIC FEATURING BUKOWSKI, OR SKID ROW INSPIRED NOISE!! VINTAGE BUKOWSKI

ODDS & ENDS

118

PART 2

BY RIKKI HOLLYWOOD

119

'Books of a Dirty old man' Part 2
by Rikki Hollywood

first became aware of Bukowski around 1983. I think I must have read an interview with him in a newspaper or something but I remember a Chinese friend mentioning him when we were talking about Raymond Carver. He said he'd first seen Bukowski on French TV, all pissed up and harassing the other 'Arty' guests before being asked to leave. He also mentioned he'd read a short story by Bukowski about someone being locked in a Zoo over night and fucking all the animals! I've not come across that story yet but it did wet my appetite for the weird and get me curious about tracking down this Bukowski fellow. I looked in local bookshops (New & Second Hand) but with no luck, then one day I was in Ladbroke Grove Library and I came across Post Office by Charles Bukowski...

POST OFFICE (Black Sparrow)
It was a tatty Alison & Busby paperback edition. It had a scubby unshaved slob-face in profile pose on the front and the word Bukowski in paint splattered writing down the side. I turned the book over to read the blurb on the back: *"A Laureate of American low-life" "Takes you by the shoulders and shakes you until your teeth rattle" "Cunningly, relentlessly, jokey and sad"* and then a brief summery of the book's world sales (Over half a million) and that Sartre has called Bukowski *"the best poet in America"* I felt like I'd

arrived really late for the party.
I opened the book and was immediately drawn in by the simple direct humour and irony of the writing from the Code of Ethics memo at the start to the reality of what it's like to be a sex crazed-gambling-drunk trying to hold a job down as a post man at Christmas. The honesty was refreshing. A sad but not self-pitying Bukowski didn't dress everything up in word play he just wrote like he spoke.

Post Office, I was to later find out, was Bukowski's first novel. He had done many books of poetry before then but this was as good a way as any for getting the decade he spent as a postal clerk off his chest. Bukowski worked for the Unite States Postal Service in Los Angeles, a job that

took no effort except for the strength to show up and the
patience to perform mindless operations. During that time,
his life bordered on insanity and death, two prevalent themes
in his writing. Im sure many people who read the book
identified with Bukowski/Chinaski's run ins especially with
tedious fellow workers and foremen like Jonstone in his
blood red shirt and brown nose attitude!

So the novels were the beginning of my Bukowski initiation
as Im sure it was for many people in the UK being as it was
easier to get the books Post office, Factotum and Women in
paperback through UK publishers such as Alison & Busby,
Virgin and Star among others, though the avid Bukowski
collector would want to get all the different editions available, these days the superior Black Sparrow edition's are the
ones to look out for first.

Post Office for instance comes in their usual distinctive large
style format. Nice to hold and easy to read with a light blue
cover showing a ripped envelope addressed to Bukowski in
California and the post mark 1970. The book came out in
1971 and at time of writing is (along with Ham on Rye)
Bukowski's most popular (and accessible) book. It's now
approaching it's 40th print and Im sure many postmen have
shlepped around the world with this in their sack, either
delivering it to avid buk fans or reading it in their lunch hour
for salvation!

FACTOTUM (Black Sparrow)

Factotum came out in 1975 published, like nearly all of
Bukowski's work, again by Black sparrow press. The dedication unlike in Post office (dedicated to nobody) was to
John and Barbara Martin, the publishers of Black Sparrow
books. John Martin remember was the man who went round
Bukowski's while he was still working at the Post Office and
offered to become his publisher full time. After a little negotiating about living expenses, a sum was agreed and
Bukowski quiet the his job to write full time. I wonder what
Jonstone would have made of it?!

But back to Factotum which see's this very entertaining second novel continue the plight of Chinaski and the various cruddy jobs and flea pit rooms that he found himself in during his travels around the depression-era states with his cardboard suit case done up with his trouser belt. He found the word 'Factotum' while thumbing through a dictionary and decided it summed up his exploits as a 'jack of all trades' during this period. We read his out bursts of writing, the stretch of job after job and cruel employment from a bicycle warehouse to janitor to auto-parts warehouse to janitor etc. The excessive drinking to get him through it. Tales of rooming houses and broken women along the way. A futile movement from one to the other, then quickly forgotten and onto the next town and more of the same.

A lot of people ask me why I read Bukowski? Isn't he depressing? Sexist? Samely? Well I think yes and no. When

your in the mood Bukowski is like a breath of fresh air. The simplicity and eye for detail in an average job and bar he's describing comes alive. Be it a ripped stocking or a drunks bulbous nose, he see's it then puts it across in a natural spontaneous way that most of us can identify with. The characters are a bit lost but this is where Sartre see's the genius of Bukowski's unrelenting honesty through facing it square on in his writing. Sometimes you wish Bukowski would try to make sense of it all but he goes one better, the world is crazy and people are crazy,
and driving themselves crazy trying to work it all out and Bukowski seems to realise this. The shitty beatings he used to take from his father, his torrid skin condition at school. The dog eat dog system that pits people against each other...all these things Bukowski realised were crazy yet he could either be an emotional cripple, seeing a shrink every week to make sense of his past...or except it as a 'bad deal' and get on with his life. Chase women that are bad for him, drink himself stupid, bet and fight and still roll into work the next day.... there is a hell of a lot of strength and resolve in ordinary people with all the shit they get thrown at them in their lives but sometimes Bukowski seems to go looking for it. But resilience is a funny thing and because it all happens bit by bit, you can't see it. If you saved it all up, all the grief and tragedy that you've handled in your life and realised you still haven't gone under you'd have the confidence of a Superman. yet something seems to get us through the day and for Bukowski (Between it all) was his writing, and in Factotum there's some of the best of it.

WOMEN (Black Sparrow)
Women was the third novel written by Bukowski. He had covered his stint at the Post Office in his first novel of the

same name. He had covered his days of aimless jobs and
hobo travelling in his second Factotum, so naturally it
seemed his third novel should be about the various crazed
women Bukowski had bedded and befriended along the way.
This content gave Bukowski a lot of material to draw from
and he laid most of it down in the near 300 pages of the
book. The Black Sparrow edition of Women has a paper bag
brown colour cover with a colour Bukowski cartoon painting of a women in suspenders/ large breasts and of course
blond hair. The Alison & Busby cover is less obvious and
shows two dirty arms (Man and Woman's) both holding
each other's hand. Half gentle/ half struggling.
The quote at the beginning by Chinaski "Many a good man
has been put under the bridge by a women" sets the tone of
the book but just to be on the safe side there's a disclaimer
on the next page saying the novel is a work of fiction and is
not meant to portray any people living or dead.
If you knew Bukowski then Im sure you would recognise
yourself somewhere in the book around this time period,
same as in his novel Hollywood where he hardly disguises
various 'Actors and Actresses' he met along the way.
So here he is, Henry Chinaski, alone for 4 years, 50 years
old, redefining Don Juan in his own sleazy way. He finds
love, and more love and with it the natural chaos that ignites
the Chinaski
legend. Some have said Bukowski must have made up his
exploits with women in his early days. Poet Harold Norse
described Bukowski as Misshapen - a big lumbering hunch-
back, with a revenged pockmarked face, decayed nicotine-
stained teeth, and pain-filled green eyes. Flat brown hair that
seemed pasted to an over sized skull - hips broader than
shoulders, hands grotesquely small and soft. A beer gut
sagging over his belt and with a ragged shirt and ill-fitting

suit like convicts receive when released, he looked like one almighty down and out! But even looking like that Bukowski can shine through. I've always said in this Sine that I like Bukowski because he's accessible, familiar, unpretentious and funny with it. And Im sure this is what women went for as well. In fact there are quiet a lot of other writers out there who cover the same subjects as Bukowski but without his style. Henry Miller springs to mind. He writes all this 'stream of conscious' sexual babble yet when you look for the person behind the essence of the feelings, there isn't anyone. Least no one you can really relate to like Bukowski. It's all or nothing and after so many pages of the Miller hero's exploits, it just becomes a monotonous and repetitive drone in colourful language but little substance.

Having said that, there are some books of poetry by Bukowski were you can sense him becoming a parody of himself and believing in his own success. Maybe Bukowski was aping his hero Hemingway, who in later life saw his writing getting weaker, flat and more obvious along with his real life escapades to match his self proclaimed image on the page.

BARFLY: The Movie (Black Sparrow)
And talking of self-made images we move onto the next Bukowski book: "Barfly" the screenplay (1987)   The actual movie Barfly was probably a lot of peoples first visual encounter with Bukowski. Bukowski did have a cameo appearance at the bar but a lot of people may have missed it and so took the Micky Rouke image as the real Bukowski, which in turn made Buk come across as a Neanderthal meathead who could barely string two words together let alone know how to hold a pen and write.
  When you look back at early pictures of Bukowski you see

a man in fairly conservative short sleeved cotton shirts, neat chino's or dark trousers and fairly respectable shiny shoes. Apart from the odd bit of stubble, he was looking like the sort of bloke you could leave alone with your sister. And this was no bad thing because when his writing was so good he didn't need to go overboard with the image. But I guess Cinema is a different medium and people wanted to see an imagined 'larger than life' Chinaski from the page not a real Bukowski from life. Even looking at the stills in the "Barfly" book we see Bukowski dressed pretty straight along side the other real Barflies from the Bar scenes.

I enjoyed the photo's in the middle of the book, shot around the movie set featuring the cast and among others David Lynch, Bukowski's wife Linda and the above mentioned various real life Barflies, but above all I enjoyed reading the screen play book more than I did watching the film. I could relate to the Chinaski character more in the writing than watching him on screen and the character description at the start of the book is very useful. I think in a way the Director, Barbet Schroeder should have understated Chinaski more, then it would have given the dialogue more resonance. Instead the lumbering, farting, belching Rouke ape image on screen detracts from Bukowski the writer. This was also the problem I found with watching some Bukowski short story adaptions at the theatre. The cliche sweaty slob in a stained vest trying to write and drink and shag loose drunk women came across as frankly a cliche to watch. It's just not the same as reading the stuff off the page and using your imagination. It's a very fine line between good writing stuff and parody. Even the sweaty character in 'Street car named desire' would be struggling as Roukes Chinaski, and probably come across more Belushi than Brando!

HOLLYWOOD (Black Sparrow)

The whole experience that surrounded the making of Barfly the movie was slowly fermenting in Bukowski's brain then finally in 1989 it was realised as the novel Hollywood. We have the usual disclaimer at the beginning 'this is a work of fiction...etc' but you couldn't help knowing that Bukowski had based a lot of the characters in the book around people he'd met during the making of the film. All thinly disguised but you don't need to be Kojak to work them out. In fact like much of his writing, with a tweak here and there he could use the book as a cathartic way of making sense of the craziness of the 'Barfly movie project' and all the Hollywood bullshit that it generated along the way. This process is much like he does with the other stuff around him in his life. Stuff like parents, drinking bars, race tracks and women were all grist for the Bukowski mill.

THE LAST NIGHT OF THE EARTH POEMS.
(Black Sparrow)

The book Last Night of the Earth Poems came out in 1992 and it was indeed a prodigious collection of poems (over 400 pages) and his first poetry collection in four years. Earth Poems is an inspired volume. Bukowski has moved through revelry into a period of remembrance of the revelry. Some of the intensity is gone, but it's replaced by thoughtful introspection and greater attention to craft. Even the photo at the back by Michael Montfort see's Bukowski in a thoughtful and reflective pose which is very in keeping with the atmosphere of the book. The title 'Last Night of the Earth Poems' might sound like Bukowski realising these may be his last words in print on this planet but he may have another batch ready for the next world! This is the way you can choose to

read Bukowski. I thought it was very interesting when
Bukowski spoke about discovering the writer Celine, reading
him and laughing while eating ritz crackers. To many, Celine
may come across as depressing and cynical yet Bukowski
found him funny in a black humoured way. Sure a lot of the
depressing views Celine held were his own perspective yet I
would suggest Bukowski liked the 'style' in which Celine
wrote and got out his despair and anger. There's different
ways to channel your rage and to Celine and Bukowski,
they used it as life used them. In fact reading 'Earth Poems'
again, you can begin to hear a more laid back Bukowski
voice in your head narrating the words as opposed to the
screaming demon from 'Love is a Dog from Hell' era.
Quantity is quality in this case and Last Night of the Earth
Poems sits high in my list of favourite Bukowski books.

BETTING ON THE MUSE (Black Sparrow)

When I first saw the horse racing cover for Betting on the
muse I thought it was going to be a collection of Bukowski
stories from the race track collected from previous works,
but it was in fact poems and stories from an archive of
unpublished work that Bukowski left to be published after
his death. If your a new reader of Bukowski this is a good a
place as any to start as the collection is poems and short
stories from, I would say between 1990 and 1994 when the
old man was at the zenith of his 'magic'. The writing is sharp
and precise with nearly every page vintage Bukowski covering all his regular subjects. The self observational poems are
also very stimulating especially the mini biog called My
Madness which pretty much puts across the Bukowski
motivation to write: '.. Maybe to put across the words I
hadn't yet read, to get the Tiger off my back' Also a very
observant poem called 'this dirty, valiant game' about how

Bukowski see's how the other poets and writers have fared down the ages from Dostoevsky and Li Po to Ginsberg, Leary, Miller, etc.
 All in all Betting on the Muse is a great read, keeping the memory of Bukowski alive and kicking with the content coming in as fresh as a winning nag. Put your money on this one!

ALL BOOKS AVAILABLE FROM: *AIRLIFT*

Tel: 0208 804 0400
UK / Europe Distribution

or

Black Sparrow Press
24 Tenth Street
Santa Rosa
CA 95401
USA

THE CAPTAIN IS OUT TO LUNCH

Charles Bukowski
Illustrated by Robert Crumb
(Black Sparrow press)

"The guy just says it right for me...it takes a strong dose of alienation to make a good artist or writer in the modern world. You can't be too well-adjusted and still have anything interesting to say"

So say's Robert crumb of Charles Bukowski. Of course it could easily have been the other way round if Bukowski read any of Crumb comics, which Im sure he must have. This book isn't the first time these two have linked up, 1983 saw Crumb add illustration to the Bukowski short story **Bring me your love** (Black Sparrow) about a man visiting his wife in a mental home with dire consequences well captured by crumb in the final picture, then in 1984 Black sparrow released **There's no business** (Black Sparrow) This Crumb / Bukowski adaption is about a stand-up comedian whose losing his touch in the clubs. In typical Bukowski fashion the main character is someone you feel sympathy for even though they have no one to blame but themselves for their misfortune.

And so 1998 saw the release in the normal Black Sparrow edition of the **Captain is out to lunch and the sailors have taken over the ship.** (It came out previously as a signed deluxe Colour limited edition book) The book itself is a first for Buk as it brings to life a journal Bukowski kept between 28th August 1991 through to 22nd February 1993. We even have the exact times of the day the entries were made as Bukowski gives us an insight into a typical Bukowski day. Going to the track, meeting the media, feeding his cats, film openings, proof readings, getting going at the computer class, even down to minute details about puking and shitting. I guess it wouldn't be a true Buk book without that detail. Hell, we even get an entry of Buk wanting to cut his toenails (9.11.91) but not finding the time! Perhaps the five minutes he spent staring at a paper clip (12.9.91) he should have spent more productively, ie. cutting his toenails!

All in all it's a good read like chatting with an old friend and Bukowski's leisurely style and humour brings it off well. The illustrations by Crumb of buk are excellent lifting different scenes from the entries such as Buk in the hot tub, Buk on the escalator seeing a friend who owed him money trying to avoid eye contact, Buk in his car on the way to the track, Buk sitting down looking at Hollywood stars in photo's that sicken him with their bland, empty faces. Yep, there's times it's vintage Buk. My only gripe is why the Buk portrait picture on the back of the book wasn't put on the cover rather than the ship? Oh well. We began with Crumb at the start of this review, here's a snatch of him talking again about Bukowski:

'One of my favourite current writers is Charles Bukowski, his stuff is generally autobiographical. Some of his best writing is from letters he writes to people. Real offhand, talking about his life. It's so great, so rich."

Available from: Airlift Dist:
0208 804 0400 (UK / Europe)

Black Sparrow press
24 Tenth Street
Santa Rosa
CA 95401
USA

LOCKED IN THE ARMS OF A CRAZY LIFE
Biography of Charles Bukowski
Howard Sounes
(Rebel Inc)

Fans of biographies be they Bukowski fans or not would do well to get hold of this book. I say this because it's an excellent example of researching a reputation. The book is well written and packed with some intimate never seen before black & white photo's of buk's old haunts, friends and family. At the start of each chapter we see Buk's familiar little man cartoons (it has to be said, not unlike the ones humorist James Thurber used to draw around his writing) and from the start Sounes is on the trail of, it seems the Bukowski myth. If you only know Bukowski through his poems and stories (which is really how most of us came across him) - then you'd do well to read this book perhaps to temper the one sidedness Bukowski can put across of his life via his alter-ego Henry Chinaski. Sounes writes clearly and consciously doing his best to track down anyone and everyone who had some kind of influence in Bukowski's life and (be warned) not all of them are as praising of the old man as you might like. I found this a refreshing change. When I finished the book I was even more pleased it wasn't as sycophantic as some of the other buk biog's I'd come across. It was also refreshing because it added another dimension to Buk.

Even his Black Sparrow publisher John Martin states the on the back, that Locked in the arms' captures clearly and truthfully the essence of Bukowski both as writer and man. Sure, it's his writing that's the most important thing and we wouldn't even be talking about the guy if it wasn't for that yet Bukowski did manage to become as interesting off the page as on it. From the drunken outburst on the french TV show that had the country going out the next day to buy up all his books, to a few years later going into restaurants to find waiters queuing up to bow to him out of respect. To have Sartre and Miller sing his praises..... did Buk make this stuff up? Who cares! Who cares because if he couldn't back it all up in his writing he'd be a nobody now. No Bukowski was the genuine article warts and all and his growing sales contest to that. At the time of writing 'Locked in the arms of a crazy life' is reprinted in Large format paperback from Rebel inc. It

retails at £10 which is a real bargain with nearly 300 pages and a great reference section at the back for other Bukowski contacts. (We no Bukowski Zine?)
Available from:
Rebel inc: 0131 557 5111

HAM ON RYE
Charles Bukowski
(Rebel Inc)

"This is a great book to learn about life, in fact lets put it on the national curriculum and give our kids a head start" (Bukowskine #3)

Bukowski's writing has staying power as will be confirmed when this book is discovered by a new generation via Rebel Inc securing UK rights and re releasing the book. Roddy Doyle states in the new introduction it was the book that put him back on track with Bukowski after 10 years away. And even if you haven't heard of Bukowski - It's really a great place to start!
For openers it's one of Bukowski's most accessible and moving books as he describes growing up in the depression. If not on the streets of Germany and the states then certainly in the home, it's recognisable in it's

imagery of alienation and bewilderment right from the opening passage of Bukowski observing adult legs from under the table. (Even then he felt better away from people than with them) This was a wise move as bukowski grows up and into a world where everybody's doing one thing and saying another. Behind the clear simple words there's also a remorseless sense of strength in the narration. Bukowski knows the truth. Truth of integrity? Who knows where the feeling comes from that won't let Buk turn a blind eye to the hypocrisy of people outside the front door or behind it in his own home. Lets face it, Bukowski trusted himself, a gut feeling he would carry with him for the rest of his life and celebrate in his writing.

His upbringing showed he could go the distance after the slings and arrows of street fights with other boys, having his acne drilled, the rejection by women, more fights, run ins with his old man about anything and everything, shitty jobs, employers in his face, more female rejection, and Bukowski just kept it up, banging out what he knew straight from the gut, taking these situations and turning them round on the page. Day after day, page after page. One of Buk's hero's Hemingway could never write a book like Ham on Rye. I sum up Hemingway in this ditty:

Hemingway (A Life)
Hemingway was a writer
who liked Bull fighting and drink,
he shot a lot of animals
then made himself extinct.

And this is true. Hemingway couldn't move on where as Bukowski had the great redeemer on his side: humour. Yes, he wrote the tough stuff but with age Bukowski had the maturity to go back and see the no bitter / sweet humour of his situation at home. Sure he's slagged off his old man in other books but no more is the situation better understood than in his novel **Ham on Rye** that his old man probably gave him his apprenticeship in writing about real feelings. I wonder how Buk would have faired if he had nobody to rebel against like the James Dean character in Rebel without a cause? Or if his old

man had of spoiled him? These are the sort of questions no doubt the Books analysing Bukowski will ask in the future, but for now we have the real thing. Rebel inc have just secured UK rights and in my opinion, (along with **Last Night of the Earth poems**) it's probably his finest moment.
Available from:
Rebel inc: 0131 557 5111
www.canongate.net

CARICATURE: NINE STORIES
Clowes, Daniel
Hot on the heels of Clowes' phenomenal GHOST WORLD success, soon to be made into a film, CARICATURE is a collection of nine dramatic short stories culled from EIGHTBALL and ESQUIRE magazine. This is his first collection since GHOST WORLD. Clowes has been described as the most respected American cartoonist after R.Crumb. A film based on GHOST WORLD will be released in 1999, directed by Terry Zwigoff and starring Christina Ricci.
FANTAGRAPHICS

Happiness
Starring: Dylan Baker, Jane Adams, Philip Seymour Hoffman
(ENTERTAINMENT IN VIDEO, CERT 18)
Investigating the dark underbelly of American picket-fence suburbia might not strike you as a particularly innovative project, but this latest audacious attempt from geeky director Todd Solondz will leave your jaw agape.

DRAWN & QUARTERLY books Reviewed available from:
Turnaround: 020 8829 3000
(Orders@turnaround-uk.com)
Also check out:
I Never Liked You / Chester Brown
The Playboy / Chester Brown
The Poor Bastard / Joe Matt
It's a Good Life, If you Don't Weaken / Seth
Best Of Drawn & Quarterly / Chris Oliveros

THE LITTLE MAN – CHESTER BROWN
Short Strips 1980-1995
Brown, Chester
The collected short strips in one edition. Featuring material produced over a fifteen year period, this book contains numerous rare and otherwise impossible to find gems that appeared in a string of longout-of-print anthologies and early issues of the classic comic book series Yummy Fur. From the wry absurdism of Dirk the Gerbil and The Gourmets From Planet X, to the restrained autobiography of Helder, virtually all of the stages in Brown's development are represented here, along with a comprehensive fourteen page section of notes.
DRAWN AND QUARTERLY

MY NEW YORK DIARY
Doucet, Julie
Doucet's third book, her longest and most ambitious story collected for the first time in one beautifully produced softcover edition. Details the events in Doucet's life during a six month period in 1991 when she packed her bags and moved to New York to join her new boyfriend in his upper west side apartment. Doucet effectively portrays how the initial excitement of their new beginning gives way to his over bearing jealousy. Includes 'My First Time' and 'Julie in Junior College'.
DRAWN AND QUARTERLY

Pages from *The Playboy* (1992), a comic about Brown's anxiety and guilt about masturbation during his teenage years; © Chester Brown

CARTOON DIARY OF JOE MATT, THE
Matt, Joe
Matt's cartoon classic in a new completely re-designed fourth printing. Peepshow documents in hilarious and sometimes painful detail the author's life during a four-year period beginning in 1987. This is by no means a 'cleansed' version of events. Here Joe Matt recounts everything from the gradual deterioration of his long and neurotic relationship with his then-girlfriend to his insatiable obsession with pornography. Funny, compelling, and ultimately tragic, this book is an excellent companion to Matt's 'The Poor Bastard'. New cover flaps and full colour endpapers.
DRAWN AND QUARTERLY

JUST THE FACTS
A Decade of Comics Essays
Collier, David
Collier tackles a broad range of subject matter in his first collection, from Thomas Edison's bygone phonograph machines to the lost art of hand lettered display ads. These strips have been culled from numerous publications, and serve as an excellent introduction to the work of this quirky and unusual talent.
DRAWN AND QUARTERLY

SEX & ROCKETS
The Occult World of Jack Parsons
Carter, John
A biography of the century's most strange men, Parsons was a primary architect of modern rocket science and co-founder of Jet Propulsion Laboratory – a crater on the moon was named after him. His secretive interests, however, were more bizarre and involved him in underwriting the notorious Aleister Crowley whose Book of the Law he considered to be the new Holy Book. Parsons also held numerous soirees where weird black magick rituals were performed under the eyes of none other than L Ron Hubbard who then made off with his money and his wife. Stranger than fiction
FERAL HOUSE

KILLER KOMIX 2
Kerekes, Slater
At last! The long awaited follow-up to the critically acclaimed first vol. From a team of top artists comes a savage and at times poignant indictment of serial killer psychosis. Several notorious crime cases are represented in adult comic strip form, deconstructing the media circus surrounding the phenomenon of the serial killer, while at the same time recognising the impact these pariahs have had on (mis)shaping the Twentieth Century.
HEADPRESS

AMOK – FIFTH DISPATCH
The Amok Sourcebook
Swezey, Stuart (ed)
Directory of the Extremes of Information in Print

SLEEPWALK
Tomine, Adrian
"Tomine works with the deft, terse strokes of a short story writer, following a small idea or a simple notion to its logical and usually poetic conclusion. He has a cinematic knack for finding the telling proper composition, the angle to capture these pensive instants, your heart skips along with those of Tomine's characters."
– New City Literary Supplement.
DRAWN AND QUARTERLY

KAFKA: GIVE IT UP & other short stories
Illustrated by Peter Kuper
(NBM)

Kafka wrote like a man detached from his body. "What do I have in common with the jews? I don't even have anything in common with myself" This quote probably expresses the essence of Kafka, a man described by his friends as living behind a 'glass wall'. Kafka tended to write in the tradition of the great Yiddish storytellers, whose stock-in-trade was bizarre fantasy, tainted with black humour and self abasement. Camus was a fan and it can be seen clearly in the almost unbearable alienated consciousness festering in Kafka's mind that later existentialism was to echo in literature. From the roots of family, Surroundings and his own body, he was confronted with the truth of his individual situation, this he in turn used to create a unique literary language in which to delve. From a hunger artist who starves himself to death in front of an audience to a giant cockroach chased from pillar to bed post in his own home. Kafka finds many varied ways to explore his dilemma of life and what it seems to throw at him. The fact that his writing was also so calm and collected add's to the power and madness it brilliantly conveys.

EYE OF THE BEHOLDER
Kuper, Peter

Started as the first comic strip ever to run in the New York times, this silent set of strips chronicles the world, its foibles, its intricacies, its dreams through the eyes of most anything you can imagine. The trick is to figure out whose eyes they are before seeing the final panel... Kuper's award winning illustration have appeared in Time, The New Yorker, Village Voice among others. With an introduction by Eric Drooker.
NBM

GIVE IT UP
And Other Short Stories
Kafka, Franz
Illustrated by Peter Kuper

Peter Kuper illustrations in **Give it up and other stories** gives us more breath taking art work improvising a selection of Kafka's short stories to great effect. The dense black and white illustrations reach down into the recess of your mind much like Kafka's writing and keep you transfixed as you find your eyes drawn from page to page. The bridge and The Top really stood out for me. I put on some Sebestyen's Marta's Hungarian folk music to add to the mood as I read the book (check out: **Ivor Cutlers 'Cute (h)ey? CD**: isbn: 1858485657 It has this track among other great atmospheric songs, he also mentions Kafka in the sleeve notes!) There's also an introduction by Jules Feiffer who likens Kupers illustrations to Jazz, a series of riffs, visual interpretations on short takes, a daring high wire act.

So here's real collectors item for any Kafka fan and hell, if your not one then buy it for someone who is. Im sure we all know someone who doesn't answer the door or pick up the phone as quickly as they used to...post it through their letter box...tell them K sent you.

Available from Turnaround: 020   8829   3000
(orders@turnaround-uk.com)

BEGINNERS GUIDE TO BUKOWSKI
Carlos Polimeni
illustrated by Miguel Rep
Writers & Readers

This makes my job a lot easier when people ask me about Bukowski. If they don't feel like reading the other two biog's, *Hank* by Neeli Cherkovski or *Locked in the arms of a crazy Life* by Howard Sounes then they can pick up this handy and lively book. It very accessible to the average reader whether your a Buk fan or not. Carlos Polimeni takes us through Buk's life in bite size chunks from his days battling at home with his mother and father, to school where he finds he has the knack to write what people like (basically what they want to believe) discovering the gods in booze, laying his old man out with a single punch, then to finally hitting the road (instead of his father) and discovering women, booze, racing, and the world along the way!

Miguel Rep's drawing's are very lively and spontaneous around the loose text and it's enjoyable recognising the photo's of Bukowski the illustrations are taken from. I think Bukowski would very much have of approved of them.
All in all you get the spontaneous feel for Bukowski from this engaging book. I open a random page, I get a Bukowski Quote:
"sex is interesting, but it's not totally important. I mean it's not even as important (physically)   as excretion. A man can go seventy years without a piece of ass, but he can die in a week   without a bowel movement"
When my friend first saw the cover of this book, she thought it was a Beginners guide to the TV show: Last of the Summer Wine. I must admit the Bukowski cover picture did look a bit like compo, it has to be said.
How about 'Last of the summer Wino's?
Available from: Writers & Readers 020 7226 2522

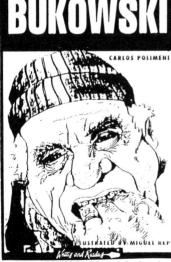

A world which, although he hated, gave him the energy and motivation to write like a demon when he got home from numerous shitty jobs.

'It's like TV show, Family Feud. Two teams play against each other, and they're not trying to figure out the *right* answer, but the *common* answer. For instance, the host will ask, "what items are in a refrigerator?" Now, in my fridge you'll find Kodak film and some obscure brand of yogurt. But that's not the right answer. The right answer is milk, butter or eggs- whatever their demographic testing has told them is the most common item. If you get those answers you win. That's the game. You're rewarded for knowing what everyone knows. Well, it's not just on *Family Feud* where your rewarded for knowing what people know. In life, you have to know what people expect you to know. Otherwise you end up in the nut house.'

And the book is full of these remarkable little gems of perceiving and understanding. I guess if your an artist you have to encapsulate what you see / feel through a visual medium (paintings or comix etc) so your mind has to distill the situation you want to put across in a non-verbal manner. Because these people have mastered that way of translating thought - when they *can* use words they can put points of view across in a very clear and simple way but with real insight like they would apply to their illustrations.

DANGEROUS DRAWINGS
Edited By Andrea Juno
Juno Books

Available from Airlift: 0208 804 0400

This book is an excellent introduction to the world of adult illustration, not only do we get to see the art work of 14 provocative, vital, boundary-breaking artists but we get to see how they tick inside with Andrea Juno asking some very pertinent questions with good follow ups from the replies. For instance, there's a cracking interview at the beginning with Art (Raw, Maus,) Spiegelman were he talks about Philip K. Dick and trying to understand other peoples sense of reality;

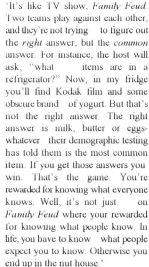

My only reservation I have about the book is the lurid pink and green cover. When I first saw it, I thought it was just a book of macho- erotic drawings like the girl on the front. It was only on closer inspection I saw the names Dan Clowes, Chris Ware, Chester Brown, Julie Doucet, Art Spegelman etc that I thought: this is actually about loads of different artists. I would hate to think the book wasn't getting picked up by comic fans because they though it was just erotic art sketches inside. Anyway, all in all its a great book and I hope Andrea Juno puts together another one soon!

Airlift 02088040400

**CARICATURE
GHOST WORLD
ORGY BOUND
LOUT RAMPAGE
PUSSEY**
Daniel Clowes
(Fantagraphics)

Welcome to the weird twisted world of thirty year old's still in a limbo world of adulthood and adolescence, Welcome to the weird twisted world of the comic industry complete with nerd and fanboy conventions, welcome to the weird twisted world of shopping malls, organised religion, Gen-x teen-angst, Cults, Garage groups, art school geeks, drop outs, sports club psycho's, in fact welcome to the real world! Anything and everything, all strains of life are here, Documents in comic strip form of life as seen and heard through eye and ear of artist / writer Daniel Clowes. Everyday observations filtered through the fertile twisted brain of one who knows, who's been there. The fact that Clowes can draw as well as he writes means he can put all this down and get it out of his system. Out of his system and straight into ours! And boy, are we glad he does! No cheap jokes for the sake of it here, just spot on observations about mannerisms and social deformities in a world gone mad, and yet (and here's the hard part) he makes it's funny. Yes, it's a cynical black humour that some days seems petty and defeatist but on other days when your in the mood- there's no better.

Ladies and gentlemen step right up and enjoy fringe elements of society at a distance. Bite size stories of dribbling Satanists or red neck neighbours you can savour from afar. On the strength of these books (Compilations from his Fantagraphic Eightball comic) he's right up there with **Robert Crumb** and deservedly so. Just get your hands on these

www.fantagraphics.com

books to see why. Start with **Lout Rampage** and work your way through to **Caricature**, watch the boy progress in his mastery of observation. It really does get better and better as we watch the Clowes eye and ear for sordid detail bringing out the best and worst in cruelty and boredom of everyday human action and conversation. And the big plus is, it's all done via the medium of comic strip cartoons. This is where it really works. As Clowes himself says when talking about the two girls he created for putting across teenage angst in **Ghost world**: 'I get away with it because it's two teenage girls having my opinions, if I had some cranky old man saying the same stuff it would seem awful. He'd be a horrible monster'. This is the attitude that prevails in Clowes work and lifts it above the normal 'I hate you, I hate the world' comics.

I don't know how far down the road Terry (Crumb) Zwigoff's film adaption of **Ghost World** is, but with Clowes on board it can't miss. I saw a movie poster by Clowes recently and, going along just on the strength of the Clowes connection saw **Happiness**. A Great film that even looked like the characters had stepped straight from the pages of eightball. Right down to the Dan Pussey lookalike in the lead role! Join the party - read these books then observe the everyday people around you...Who needs fiction!

All books available from Turnaround: 020 8829 3000 (orders@turnaround-uk.com)

"Art School Confidential" from *Orgy Bound* (1996).

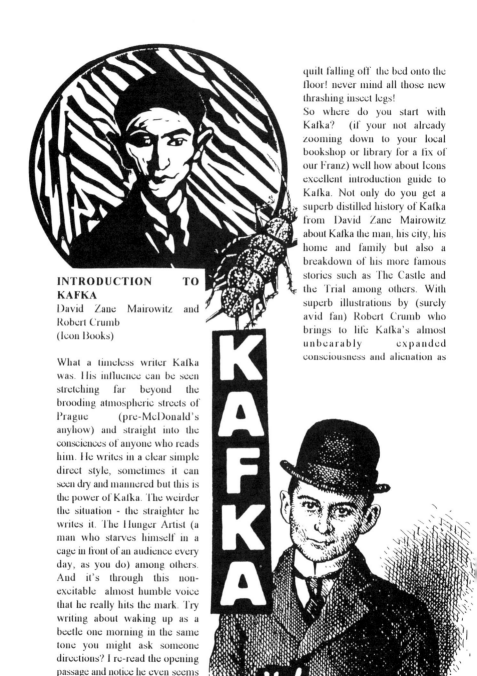

INTRODUCTION TO KAFKA
David Zane Mairowitz and Robert Crumb
(Icon Books)

What a timeless writer Kafka was. His influence can be seen stretching far beyond the brooding atmospheric streets of Prague (pre-McDonald's anyhow) and straight into the consciences of anyone who reads him. He writes in a clear simple direct style, sometimes it can seen dry and mannered but this is the power of Kafka. The weirder the situation - the straighter he writes it. The Hunger Artist (a man who starves himself in a cage in front of an audience every day, as you do) among others. And it's through this non-excitable almost humble voice that he really hits the mark. Try writing about waking up as a beetle one morning in the same tone you might ask someone directions? I re-read the opening passage and notice he even seems even more concerned about the quilt falling off the bed onto the floor! never mind all those new thrashing insect legs!
So where do you start with Kafka? (if your not already zooming down to your local bookshop or library for a fix of our Franz) well how about Icons excellent introduction guide to Kafka. Not only do you get a superb distilled history of Kafka from David Zane Mairowitz about Kafka the man, his city, his home and family but also a breakdown of his more famous stories such as The Castle and the Trial among others. With superb illustrations by (surely avid fan) Robert Crumb who brings to life Kafka's almost unbearably expanded consciousness and alienation as

he transforms himself into ape, cockroach, dog and mole via his writing. These imaginings perhaps were easier to stomach for Kafka than having to put on the front as a well adjusted human being in a crazy world.
**Available from:
Icon Books: 01763 208 008**

This wasn't the only time Kafka would arrange to have himself SENTENCED TO DEATH. It had to be that way. Suicide wasn't in the cards.

But Death itself took too long. For Kafka, there would always be another way: making himself "DISAPPEAR".

There were many variants on this theme, although it would always be a matter of making himself SMALL. His existence, as such, was an offence against nature. He saw himself as an object, for example, a wooden clothes-rack, pushed into the middle of the room.

Or: "A picture of my existence ... would show a useless wooden stake covered in snow ... stuck loosely at a slant in the ground in a ploughed field on the edge of a vast open plain on a dark winter night."

THE LIFE & HAZARDOUS TIMES OF CHARLES BUKOWSKI
CD Audio Book
(Chrome Dreams/Enlightenment)

Along with various written biographies of Bukowski, we now have an audio version where we hear snippets of the man himself talk about his life. The CD breaks Bukowski life down into eight segments from the emotionally deprived childhood and beating by his father, through teenage problems with acne and alleged draft dodging, through the joys of drink and the racetrack to menial jobs, crazy lovers, and finally quitting the Post Office to concentrate on writing full time and performing poetry. Finally he finds success in the small press meets Linda Lee Beighle, grows ever more popular in Europe, has stories adapted into movies and buys a BMW. Listening to the CD we get to hear Bukowski reminisce about these various stages of his life with a certain indifference and we can't help thinking: if he was a character in one of his own stories, he would have ended up a lot worse at the finishing post than he, in reality, did but then having heard the mans life laid out then read the quotes from buk insert booklet: 'I fear life more than I fear death' 'Some people never go crazy. what truly horrible lives they must lead' 'Wisdom is doing what the crowd does not do' we then get an idea of how Bukowski got through life. He trusted himself.
CD Available from: Chrome Dreams: 0208 715 9781

YOUR VIGOUR FOR LIFE APPALLS ME
Robert Crumb Letters 1958-1977
(FANTAGRAPHICS)
THE R. CRUMB COFFEE TABLE BOOK
Knockabout
CRUMB FAMILY COMICS
(Last Gasp)

"...the only burning passion I have is the passion for sex" so said an early letter Crumb sent to his friend among many others when describing his life. Those friends it seems have hung onto these letters and now they see the light of day in chronological order from 1958 to 1977 for our delectation. the correspondence in **'Your vigour for life appalls me'** littered with early crumb sketches span the most important part of his life, from the painful formative years of his early adolescence to the fame and fortune of his adulthood, describing bitter struggle and ultimate triumph as being regarded as the greatest cartoonist of the 20th century. Along with this book also check out **Crumb Family Comics** and **The R. Crumb coffee table book** these also show us the early stages of Crumbs progress as he meanders through life trying to find a voice for his art. From sending off Fritz the cat cartoons to Harvey Kurtzman while working at a greetings card company to getting a leg up the ladder via the hippy movement in the 60's where Crumb could now let his chemical mind run loose to like minded spaced out LSD souls.

In all three books we see how Crumb developed as an artist by sticking by what he liked (Truth, sex & old blues records) eventually after the 60's were over he moved into his greatest asset his 'own mind'. Without drugs Crumb was even more of a unique voice. He hated capitalism, the Disney-fication of everything, the synthetic over the real. For all the slating crumb has taken over being sexist and racist you always felt Crumb (like Bukowski) was his own man. His

crazed cartoonist has to kick in and bring a bit of chaos back to things. Not that he didn't have his share before hand, dip anywhere into **Crumb Family Comics** and you'll be surrounded in a world of dysfunctional family art. It's in this book we learn more about his brother Charles. Check out the minute scribbles on the inside cover that Charles used to fill note book after note book with. At the end of the book and movie I found Charles to be not only the most likeable but also the most interesting of the Crumbs. (The CRUMBS, Jesus, was ever a name more apt!!)

So, all in all, if you want to know where the seeds sprung from that brought forth Devil Girl, Mr Natural, Fritz the cat, Snoid, and the mind of the best autobiographical comic writing ever, then these books are where to start.
ISBN: 1560973102
Available: TURNAROUND DIST: 0181-881-5088

own worse enemy? Perhaps, but then the energy has to come from somewhere and be channelled, what better way if you can draw as intensely as you feel! Perhaps it's yin & yang effect. Crumb *the family man* feels complacent with comfort (The nice house, the wife and daughter) so crumb *the*

EL BORBAH
Burns, Charles
Meet El Borbah, a four hundred pound private eye who wears Mexican wrestlers tights and an eerie mask. Subsisting entirely on junk food and beer, El Borbah conducts his investigations with tough talk and a short temper. He smashes through doors and skulls as he stalks a perfectly re-alised film-noir city filled with punks, geeks, business suited creeps and other would be he-roes. This is the first of a collec-tors series of hardcover titles in five volumes reprinting acclaimed cartoonist Burns' ouvre up to his current magnum opus, the ongo-ing BLACK HOLE.
FANTAGRAPHICS

BIG BABY
Burns, Charles
The hugely popular Big Baby sto-ries collected in one deluxe volume for the first time. This is the second of a hardcover series of four vol-umes reprinting the entirety of Burns' oeuvre up to his current mag-num opus BLACK HOLE. Features every piece of BB comics and art available, and features brand new covers, endpapers, and over a dozen pages of never-before seen BB illustrations.
FANTAGRAPHICS

Check out more
great titles!
www.fantagraphics.com

THE BIG BOOK OF WEIRDOS
By Carl Posey & 67 of the world's top comic artists
(Paradox Press)

A stunning collection of Artists and Oddballs who include Ed Wood Jr, Kafka, William Burroughs, Hitler, Poe, Idi Amin, and Wilhelm Reich among many others.
Their lives and acts perfectly encapulated in these black and white four to six page comic strips that actually display their outlandish impulses right down to the mad eyes and sweating brow. Dip into any page and see the other side of the coin of genius & madness at work. **Airlift Dist: 0208 804 0400**

CALLING THE TOADS
A William Burroughs compendium
Published by Ring Tarigh

William Burroughs was the father of the modern beats changing the landscape of underground writing with his classic novel Naked Lunch. Junkie, artist, innovator of the 'cut up & fold in' method of writing and an influence to just about every bugger who stumbled across him between then and now. This book contains just such people. The main content of the book is question / answer interviews with Burroughs along with selected essays. You'll find on the other end of pen and phone are such people as Gordon ball, Douglas (majic bus) Brinkley and Allen Ginsberg. Interspersed throughout are various black & white photos of Burroughs at home, doing readings, even sitting in a sauna with other OAP playmates. Because Burroughs is so interesting your lead on page after page hoping he'll come out with something not unlike a revelation. He comes close a few times but as with taste, you'll have to find your own favourite answers. All in all it's another 'Burroughs tribute' book but well worth getting if not just for the strange Autopsy feature at the end (The Nature of the death is clear. A bullet through the forehead. The evidence shows that the couple were communicating at the point when the missile entered the forehead, leading to a suspicion that they were both conscious of the likely outcome. Or was it all just a drunken prank that went wrong. As Mr. B says: we have a destiny.) Your's dear reader will be to get hold of this book if your a fan of the unhinged. The cover shows a great early morning stroll photo of 'Old Bill' out 'Calling all the toads" to follow him home no doubt...
ISBN: 0965982602
Available: TURNAROUND DIST: 0181-881-5088

GHASTLY TERROR
The Horrible Story of the Horror Comics
Sennitt, Stephen
Traces the development of comics from the gross psychotic visions of the ultra-primitive 'pre-code' horrors, through to the relatively sophisticated graphic nightmares of Warren and Skywald. Fully illustrated throughout, this is a concise, entertaining and enlightening examination of this most popular and persecuted of comicbook genres.
HEADPRESS Turnaround Dist(UK)

FOUR WALLS EIGHT WINDOWS

Art © Robert Crumb

NEW AMERICAN SPLENDOR ANTHOLOGY
BOB & HARV'S COMICS
OUR CANCER YEAR
Harvey Pekar
four walls eight windows

Recognition for Pekar's sublime self published comic 'American Splendour' has long been over due. Every time your trusty reviewer used to find himself in one of London's trusty comic shops and ask for it, the reply back was the usual resounding: WHO?! Never heard of him!
But I wasn't put off, and one way or another I managed to track down at least 5 or 6 of these wonderful comics. Then suddenly, Turnaround link up with publisher's Four walls Eight windows and you can now savour Harvey for yourself with these three graphic novel collections of his work.
Well I say Harvey's work, all the writing is Harvey's (such as his life of being a Hospital records porter, girl friend hassles, paying the rent, thinking about life, even buying a loaf of bread!) But the illustrations are by different artists. Where these stories stand up to reading and re-reading is that they don't have any punch lines or twists in the tail, they aren't your usual Superhero or druggy underground comic. They are just the everyday thoughts or actions that your average person makes. It's in the minute detail of everyday life that Harvey shines. John Lennon (I think) said life is what happens to you while your making other plans, well Harvey captures those 'moments' so well and it's all here page after page. And they are brutally honest too. Good and bad, Harvey opens up and you get the full Monty. I was going to review these books individually but, like Harvey's life, they are a collective. All part of the same story. Living in Cleveland, meeting Robert Crumb in the early day's when he was illustrating greeting cards and sharing a love for old records, to finally getting him to draw and bring to life Pekar's first attempted stick men story. He did and Pekar didn't look back. Car trouble, friend trouble, selling records, stealing records, making a buck here and there, just getting by! I think Bukowski would have liked this comic because Pekar rages against the system yet see's his his own fallibility as well. It borders on the 'exotic' said Robert Crumb in a forward and he's right, it's exotic in it's normalness yet in the average comic shop with shelves groaning under the weight of more super hero bullshit that's a positive plus. It's in a class of it's own. Do yourself a favour and discover Harvey Pekar Today!!

**All books available from:
Turnaround: 020 8829 3000
(Orders@turnaround-uk.com)**

DISTURBINGLY DARK, SWEETLY SAVAGE!!!

BACK EDITIONS OF HEADPRESS JOURNAL

Headpress 18	£8.50
Headpress 15–17	£4.95 each
Headpress 13	£4.95
Headpress 12	£3.75
Headpress 9–12	£3.50 each

P&P each edition: UK £0.55 / Eur £1.25 / ROW £2.50

Monies payable: 'Headpress'. Mail order only.
Headpress, 40 Rossall Avenue, Radcliffe,
Manchester, M26 1JD, Great Britain
Email: david.headpress@zen.co.uk

A two-edition sub to Headpress (postage paid) is: UK £16 / Eur £18 / ROW £20

Current subscription holders also get 10% off new Critical Vision books on publication

More pages! More Mischief!

Ultra Flesh vol 1 £10.99
Cannibal Holocaust £13.99
p&p £1.70 each
Send 1st class stamp or IRC for our full catalogue of new and collectible books

BOOKS FROM CRITICAL VISION

Ghastly Terror! (pub: Sept 99)	£12.95
Killer Komix 2 (pub: Nov 99)	£8.95
Bizarrism	£11.95
Psychotropedia	£15.95
Sex Murder Art	£11.95
Intense Device	£10.95
Critical Vision	£11.95

P&P each book: UK £1.55 / Outside UK please enquire

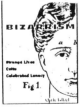

Alan Moore . Eddie Campbell
eddie campbell comics

FROM HELL

www.topshelfcomix.com

From Hell is a book to savour, to read slowly while simultaneously digesting the art work through your moist slithering eyeballs. From Hell throws us back in time to Victorian London a time of Jack the Ripper, Masonic ritual and monarchy madness. What lifts this above other 'cult of Ripper' adaptions is the way the pace of the book builds and the staggering research done by writer Alan Moore on London architecture and books / Plays of eighteenth-century London. (Not only are you entertained but you get a darn interesting history lesson to boot)
Moving effortlessly from queens chamber to the slum streets of the east end we are swept along via stage coach to pub to alley way to morgue, watching & witnessing the dirty work of ...
.Well we won't give it away here, lets just call him Jack.
Well chosen to complement Moores writing are the dark moody black & white atmospheric illustrations of artist Eddie Campbell. Through out the book they are spot on (If this book is ever turned into a film, the director has the best story board going!)
From Hell will move you, in fact if you want to go a step further - read it by candle light,...alone!

Before his death, Bukowski sent several poems and short stories to Pat Moriarity (via Dennis Eichhorn) to create comicstrip interpretations of. Most of them appear in Pat's comicbook **Big Mouth**, published by Fantagraphics Books, 7563 Lake city way NE , Seattle WA 98115 USA. Write them for a free catalogue or order **Big Mouth** comics toll free! 1-800-657-1100. *(Big mouth is now up to issue 7, but Buk's stories are in issues #1-4, and also in Fantagraphic's Zero Zero #1.)*

COCKROACH PAPERS
Richard Schweid
Four Walls Eight Windows

'Know you enemy' is a famous saying and this book is one way Bukowski could have dealt with these common little blighters in all those cheap rooms and flop houses he used to find himself in.
I read this book in bed which wasn't a good idea. Every little itch or noise then became a frantic search for cockroaches, this is the effect they have on people. Don't just take my word for it, read this book and learn more than you ever wanted to know about the insect that frightens and disgusts millions. It covers them in all stages from life to art. For instance from Kaka's Metamorphous we find Kafka didn't want to say which insect Gregor turns into, he wanted to leave it as just an *insect* - so his readers could decide for themselves how they saw him. His publishers used a cockroach on the cover and thus he was forever a Cockroach. Interesting. Then we find how exterminators work or that five thousand species of cockroach have been discovered and more are on the way! There's some great photos including a cockroaches dissected brain called a superesophagel ganglion (in case it comes up as a question in a pub quiz) also we see some Cockroach antennae fencing to sexually receptive male cockroach's getting into a bit of wing-raising then inviting the female to mount...there's even a mini cockroach flick book at the back. All in all it's a curious book but a real treat for the lover of things unusual.
Hang on. What's that scratching noise... **?!**
Available from: Turnaround dist:
020 8829 3000

THE HORRIBLE STORY OF THE HORROR COMICS
by STEPHEN SENNITT

Turnaround Dist(UK)
0208 829 3000

Back in the 1950s, horror comics flourished to the extent that some 50 or more different titles could be published in a single month. Then these comics were effectively banned, indicted as a major cause of 'juvenile delinquency' in the US and in Great Britain. Prurient themes and imagery incorporating scantily clad women, torture, limb-chopping, and trauma to the eye, were amongst those cited as objectionable and outlawed.
But what were these horrible horror comics *really like*? What were the stories about? How many titles were produced? And were they as frightening and as subversive as their critics made out?
For the first time in book form, **GHASTLY TERROR!** addresses and answers all these questions — and more! Tracing their development from the grotesque, psychotic visions of the ultra-primitive 'pre-code' horrors, through to the relatively sophisticated graphic nightmares of Warren and Skywald, **GHASTLY TERROR!** takes the reader into a dank and sinister world to savour the rotting history of TALES FROM THE TOMB, DARK MYSTERIES, WEIRD TERROR, VAULT OF HORROR, WORLDS OF FEAR, WEB OF EVIL, TALES OF VOODOO, PSYCHO, SCREAM, CREEPY, TWISTED TALES, TABOO and countless other comic titles!
Profusely illustrated throughout, **GHASTLY TERROR!** is a concise, entertaining and enlightening examination of this most popular and persecuted of comicbook genres.

PO Box 30, St. Annes on the Sea, FY8 1RL England.
Tel. +44 (0)1253 712453 Fax. +44 (0)1253 712362
e-mail: king@visicom.demon.co.uk
http://www.state51.co.uk/state51/visionary/

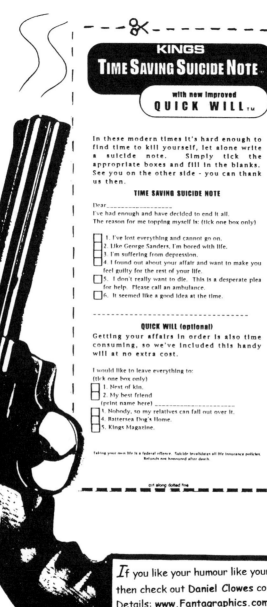

Cool Contacts!

Airlift Distribution: (Bukowski USA Black Sparrow, City Lights books & more!)
Www.nowbooks.co.uk
Turnaround Distribution: (Great list of UK & USA counter-culture books, graphic novels)
www.turnaround-uk.com
The Bukowski check list! email: **Bukzine@aol.com**
or write c/o PO Box 11271, London, N22 8BF, Great Britain for a free monthly Bukowski check list featuring latest Bukowski books, CD's Video's, tapes available or to be released. Updated every month - get on board!
*Publishers! Send Bukowski Journal any new Bukowski items for review!
Byron (London based Photographer, Web Designer, very competitive rates!)
Byronuk.co.uk
Headpress: (website of Sex Religion Death & other strange & bizarre books to order)
http://www.headpress.com
No Exit press: (Classic Crime Books including Ed Bunker, Charles Willeford,)
www.noexit.co.uk
Visionary Video's (Crime, Punk, Screen edge, Cult & Experimental Video's)
http://www.state51.co.uk/state51/visionary/
Fantagraphics (American Publishers of Crumb, Clowes, Burns, Love & Rockets etc)
www. Fantagraphics.com
Drawn & Quarterly (Comic publishers of Chester Brown, Adrian Tomine, Joe Matt, etc)
www.hardboiledegg.com/quarterly
Marion Boyars (Publishers of Hubert Selby Jr, George Bataille & lots more experimental)
Www.marionboyars.co.uk
 Calder Books (UK Publishers of Samuel Beckett, Celine, Robbe-Grillet,Trocchi, etc)
http://paris-anglo.com/calder
Ocean Bookshop (Excellent London based second hand / pulp Bookshop. Let me know what titles you want! **Phone Vince on: 0207 502 6319**
Millenium Books: (Philip K. Dick & other classic Sci-Fi books!)
For the latest list e-mail us: smy@orionbooks.co.uk
King mob: (Cult CD's like Bukowski, Ken Kesey, Nick Cave, Ken Campbell, etc)
www.king-mob.co.uk
Chrome Dreams (Biog CD's of Bukowski, the Beats, Drug writers etc)
www.chromedreams.co.uk
Paupers press (**Colin Wilson** specialist plus huge new and second hand book list!)
http://members.aol.com/stan2727uk/pauper.htm
Writers & Readers (Beginners guides to Bukowski, Kerouac, Sartre, & lots more!)
Www.writersandreaders.com
Compendium Bookshop (Londons best Bukowski / Beat shop, Video's tapes, books!) Phone Compendium on: **0207 485 8944 or 0207 267 1525**
Beat Scene (great magazine on Ginsberg, Burroughs, Bukowski, Kerouac,& more!)
Www.connectotel.com/beatscene
Bookshop @Queens (Massive array of Bukowski items from Ireland's #1 Buk shop!)
Www.baq.co.uk
Knockabout: (R. Crumb, Freak Bros, Underground Comix and distribution etc)
www.knockabout.com
R.obert Crumb's modern primitives Band (Banjo, flute, accordian,vibraphone -very exotic CD with great Robert Crumb art!) Details: sketch@easynet.fr

Bukowski Wallpaper